A GIFT IN HONOR

OF THE

SONS AND DAUGHTERS

OF ISRAEL

————————————

THE WINNICK FAMILY FOUNDATION

CRYING FOR IMMA

Battling for the Soul on the Golan Heights

Published by Night Vision Press, Los Angeles, California

©1999 by Hallie Lerman

Library of Congress Catalog Card Number
98-073170

ISBN 0-9665722-0-3

 Blueprint, San Francisco

Printed in Korea

Night Vision Press
10573 West Pico Blvd. #14
Los Angeles, California 90064

CRYING FOR IMMA

Battling for the Soul on the Golan Heights

Written and Photographed by Hallie Lerman

War Photographs by the Soldiers Who Fought

NIGHT VISION PRESS

*To You — My Guide and Inspiration
on this Journey*

A Noble Spirit of Numinous Light

CONTENTS

xi   Introduction

xiv   Principal Figures

xv   Map of the Golan Heights

1   Chapter One .... *Spoils of War*

13   Chapter Two .... *Jacob through the Eyes*

23   Chapter Three .... *Erev Yom Kippur, 1973*

57   Chapter Four .... *Scattered Pieces*

65   Chapter Five .... *The War Begins*

95   Chapter Six .... *The War Escalates*

107   Chapter Seven .... *The Land of the Dead*

131   Chapter Eight .... *Death*

147   Chapter Nine .... *Desperation*

167   Chapter Ten .... *The Tension is Breaking Us All*

177   Chapter Eleven .... *Rescue*

191   Chapter Twelve .... *Recovery: The Year Following the War*

205   Chapter Thirteen .... *War Reflections: 25 Years Later*

233   Chapter Fourteen .... *Jacob*

246   Epilogue

248   Biographies

252   Glossary

254   Acknowledgements

*I will gather you from the peoples
and assemble you out of the countries
where you have been scattered and
I will give you the land of Israel.*

—Ezekiel 11:17

INTRODUCTION

IN THE FAR NORTHERN CORNER OF ISRAEL lies a small plateau of land that rises majestically above the Hula Valley, Israel's fertile farm land. After climbing steep, meandering roads through mountainous terrain, one comes to an uneven stretch of land that extends north towards Syria. This is the Golan Heights.

Israel secured this strategic area during the Six Day War in 1967, following Syria's failed attempt to destroy the State. Since then, the Golan Heights has played a key part in Israel's security and has served as a buffer to prevent a Syrian invasion through Israel to the Mediterranean Sea. But on October 6, 1973, Yom Kippur, the Syrian forces mounted an assault. A few Israeli soldiers, garrisoned at a small outpost called Tel Saki, stood in their way. This attack, the first battle in the Golan Heights, became a microcosm of the war, a war that changed the face and character of Israel and her people.

This book describes the human face of war through photographic essays and personal interviews. It is about the soldiers whose fate bound them to a small mountain of volcanic rock.

One of those soldiers was Jacob Rayman, my cousin. Though we rarely saw each other, we were deeply connected. Each time we would meet, it would seem as if no time had passed, as if we had lived the other's life. Silence communicated private thoughts and feelings. We instinctively and intuitively knew each other.

In 1973, as a young woman, I was travelling in Israel a month before the war. Jacob begged for a leave from his army duty and received a 24-hour pass. We stayed up talking until four in the morning. When we knew we had to part, he walked me to my room. We gave each other a hug, then he walked away. Just as he was about to disappear from my view, he turned around and we looked at each other one last time. Suddenly, an aura of strange light surrounded him. I froze, stunned. "I am never going to see him again," I thought. I entered my bedroom, agitated, nervous, too tense to fall asleep. When war broke out one month later, I knew Jacob was dead.

Jacob's death was not heroic. He did not win medals. He was not cited for bravery. He died like so many others during war. He followed orders. As a medic, he knew he would serve on the front line. He was called. He went.

His memory and spirit are the inspiration behind this book. His father, Morty Rayman, supported this project from the beginning, giving me names of people to interview. Jacob's sister spoke reluctantly. Jacob's mother, Ruth, opposed.

One should never judge another during the grieving process or by how they deal with loss and sorrow, especially a parent grieving for the loss of his or her child. Grief is like a permanent rip that assaults the thin membrane of the eye, which coats itself against the onslaught of the world. A searing vision becomes the lens through which the world is felt.

As they prepare for battle, Israeli soldiers hold to the belief that their officers will safeguard their lives; they are assured that the Israel Defense Forces (IDF) will do whatever is necessary to rescue them. Israeli soldiers know they face overwhelming odds and fight with everything they have, all the more because of this solemn trust. Most importantly, they fight for Eretz Israel, the Land of Israel. They fight to preserve God's covenant with the Jewish people—that this land of Israel, their home, shall forever belong to them.

After researching historical material and interviewing others who wrote on this war, I saw that the personal and human side of the war had not yet been told. Using photographs with text, I hope to convey a sense of the combatants' experience. Instead of focusing on an entire war, I have concentrated on one specific battle as soldiers do, so that their experiences become more immediate and personal. The universal becomes known only by understanding its details. These photographs and their accompanying essays are as critical to the book as the primary text, helping readers to comprehend the war as they reflect upon the battle. By understanding the effects of one immeasurable loss, readers can discern what happens to a family, a society, to a world at large, long after the war has ended, daily life has resumed, time has passed.

Hearing about this battle from the soldiers who fought and the family members of soldiers who fell, readers will discover that each experienced the battle differently. Each survived differently, too.

In 1973, the State of Israel came close to defeat, and the soldiers at Tel Saki knew it. Each soldier spoke from his heart, sharing his fear that during the battle, the war was lost. In retelling their stories, many wept. Some withdrew into silence. One dropped his head, as if in silent prayer. Another soldier did all three.

The Battle of Tel Saki. It was comparatively small. But, for some of the soldiers who fought, their stories brought forth images of Biblical proportion. Isaac's blindness described the vulnerable position of the IDF. King David's betrayal was repeated in the arrogance of government officials who made decisions with devastating consequences. There was Joseph's dream and foresight. Jacob's struggle. Jonathan's loyalty. Abraham's faith. And Caleb's devotion mirrored Jacob Rayman's love for the Land of Israel.

This battle disintegrated into near-failure, despair, and the controlled terror of scared men. It was a battle of a few against many, and of chance victory snatched from crushing defeat.

The Golan Heights. The place where Jacob and other soldiers fell.

The Battle of Tel Saki. It is each of our battles.

Hallie Lerman
Los Angeles, California
March 1998

PRINCIPAL FIGURES

JACOB RAYMAN'S FAMILY

Mortimer "Morty" Rayman
Jacob's father

Hava Rembrand
Jacob's sister

Simhona Weber
Jacob's sweetheart and fellow soldier

Gideon Ginossar
Jacob's best friend

COMMANDING OFFICERS

Avigdor Kahalani
Tank battalion commander

Yair "Yaya" Yoram
Jacob's battalion commander

Itzhak Kahane
Jacob's company commander

Meir Brukenthal
Platoon leader in Jacob's company

SOLDIERS ORDERED TO TEL SAKI

Menachem Amsbacher
Jacob's commanding officer

Eliezer Agasi

Shlomo Avital

Roni Hertzenstein

Shaya Levy

FIRST ARMORED CARRIER

Binyamin "Benny" Hanni and other soldiers

SECOND ARMORED CARRIER

Yair Farjun

Jacob Rayman and other soldiers

RESCUERS

Pinchas Berkovitch

Eshel Ehud

Issac Nagarker

RELATIVES OF SLAIN SOLDIERS

Rivkah Ben Ahron
Benny Hanni's sister

Hanna Eliraz
Roni Hertzenstein's sister

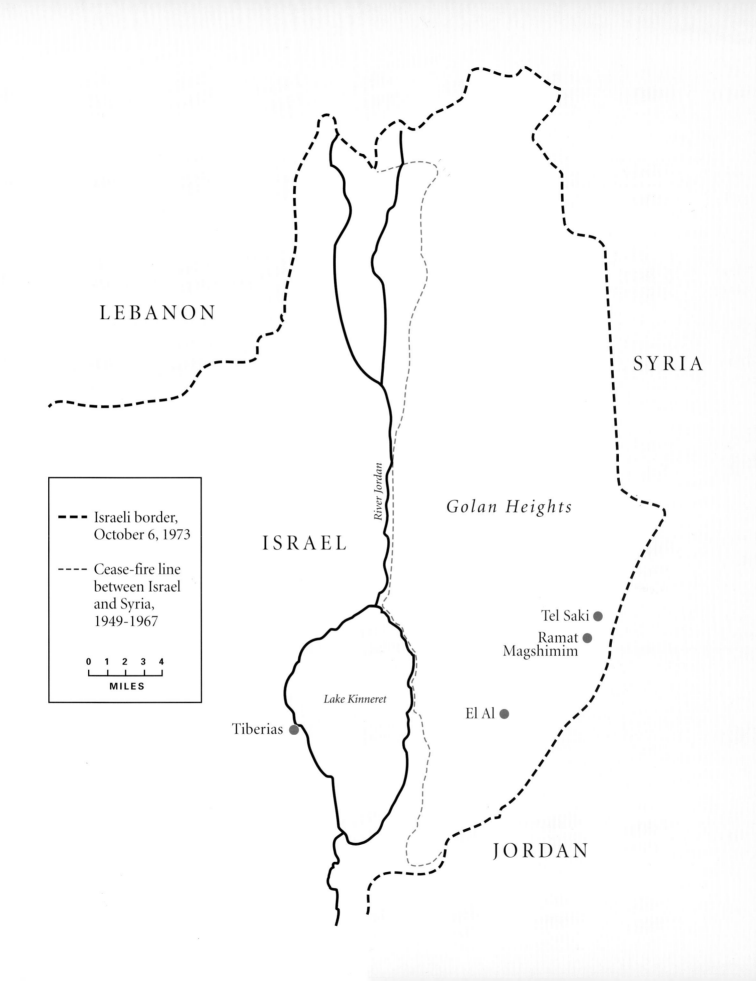

LEBANON

SYRIA

River Jordan

Golan Heights

ISRAEL

Israeli border,
October 6, 1973

Cease-fire line
between Israel
and Syria,
1949-1967

0 1 2 3 4
MILES

Tel Saki ●

Ramat
Magshimim ●

Lake Kinneret

El Al ●

Tiberias ●

JORDAN

Be strong and of good courage
Be not afraid
Neither be dismayed
For the Lord Your God is with you
Wherever you go.

— Joshua 1:9

Chapter One

S P O I L S   O F   W A R

Seven brothers surround two sisters and the seated matriarch. They stare at me like ghosts. Their futures loom ahead. Families to support. Children not yet born. Money to be made. And I stare back, knowing their future and the future of their heirs. Third from left, back row, is Jacob's grandfather. Tall, handsome Jack.

Jack. You do not know that you will die young. That your brilliant son Morty will win a full scholarship to Harvard during the time when there was a quota on Jews. Or that your grandson Jacob, your namesake, will fall in war at 19 years old. You knew that ancient land as Palestine. Jacob knew it as Israel. Jews wander. Your father journeyed from Russia. Settled in America. Your only son moved to Israel. And your grandson died where I now stand. How strange. I am foresight. I know your future. You gaze at me, confidant. Strong. Poised.

I stare back. What fools we are.

What fools.

Jacob. Are you here? My words break into broken Hebrew letters, as they are tossed and carried by the wind, shaken, thrown like dice. I remember back— before the constant shelling, the shuffling boots against the hot, loud gravel, the repetitious machine guns that kept firing and jangling your nerves. I hear an abandoned, muffled cry. The air is dusty and chalky. Sweat sticks like wet glue underneath your helmet. It is in this immediate second, not knowing who will live and who will die, that I begin to pray. Dear God. Let Jacob know once again your black, still night and wide desert sands, your luminous stars and radiant moon. Let him hear his sweetheart's voice once more, with her promises of love. Let him hear me praying out loud to You. And then I hear His answer. I feel only the wind. An awful silence.

The arid land stretches into its Biblical past, as Jacob stands tall, strong, full of life like the eucalyptus trees behind him. Energetic, outgoing, full of contagious adventure and humor, Jacob smiles confidently at the camera. He has taken his army medic training with seriousness of purpose. He knows he wants to be a doctor and follow in the footsteps of his father, the man he admires most in the world. He practices his newfound skills on every soldier in his unit. No one escapes his needle. No one can refuse his steady hands and kind, yet firm, request.

Every beloved son is exceptional to his parents. And Jacob's parents are no different. But Jacob was no ordinary son. He was the best Israel had to offer. The brightest of the bright. The most handsome of the handsome. He believed and loved deeply. A devoted son and sweetheart, a fine soldier, Jacob was focused, practical, idealistic.

Often a child is idealized by his parents once he no longer is alive. But in this particular case, the collective memory of Jacob is supported by so many who knew him. All agree he was exceptional. It is remarkable that his legacy is so sharp, that others still speak about him with such clarity and sadness, a quarter of a century later.

Ghosts loom in this abandoned, barren landscape. The years have not camou-flaged their presence. Nor has fear left the bullet-riddled bunker. Buried beneath the ground, a new bunker has been built. The phoenix rises again.

No one comes anymore to visit his lost youth. The IDF occasionally will invite a veteran to speak to new recruits about Tel Saki. To them it is ancient history. The Yom Kippur War is not their war. Reserves sometime make the journey and share the story, but this too is haphazard and impulsive. For the most part, the story has been relegated to footnotes in officer training schools. But to the families, the deaths of their fallen sons have only become harder to accept, more difficult to endure.

The soldiers' spirits lie in wait. Winds bring chilled rain, as memory is stirred from its rusty locks. Their fleeting, weightless souls remind me of their fallen fate. They travel like the crisscross veins on an upturned palm. Weeds bend over. Twigs snap back. Brush sighs as rocks take note.

Silhouettes. Profiles. Soulful moments experienced in the pause before the sigh. Soft muted grays with pastels woven through like sunset highlights. What do we remember? Do we only include the ache, the sad longing, the betrayal, the loneliness? What about the rage and the regret? Do we only see our side? The hurt done to us? Do we ever want to see the other? Is it even possible? Music we remember becomes the soundtrack of our lives. Memories the record.

O shooting star
That fell into my eyes
And through my body—
Not to forget you
To endure.

—Rainer Maria Rilke

Chapter Two

JACOB THROUGH THE EYES

Jacob's beautiful eight-year-old face, with his delicious cheeks for kissing, gazes at the camera. A Davy Crockett coonskin cap sits upon his head, a bandanna around his neck. Another costume. Another image. A real leather cowboy hat with a bright red bandanna. The same gaze with the same direct, dark brown eyes looking back.

These are the pictures of him that are most vivid to me now. Ruth loved to dress him up in costumes. I remember more about him as a little boy than as a young man. This may be true of all parents. You are so involved with your firstborn.

It feels like we had Jacob for a second. We are blessed to have had him for the short time that we did. We feel privileged to have known him for even these years. He was only 19 years old. To us, his life feels like a sky-rocket, a roman candle. Swish. We do not remember anything of him as a teenager. He was gone. In high school he was always involved with his band. Then the army took him away.

1955. Plywood built into a makeshift playpen in the back seat of a Chevrolet station wagon carries a crying baby as the family prepares for a camping trip in the British Columbia woods. Jacob's swollen eyes overflow with tears. Why does he cry so much?

Today, we realize that he wanted to do things he was just unable to do. Jacob always wanted to go further than his physical or mental development would allow him. He was a difficult baby. Impossible. You could not make him happy. So he made our lives miserable in the first year. How hard it all seemed at the time. And now? It was nothing. Nothing.

1971–1972. A very handsome young man, over six feet tall, a few inches taller than his father and a head taller than his grandfather, bounds into the room. It seems as if this is the order, the way generations should go. His charismatic presence demands attention. He eagerly puts down his uzi, unloads his burden. "Daddy," he says. "Fill me up with information."

It gave me tremendous joy and satisfaction that he was proud of me as a doctor and wanted to be a doctor like me. I was extremely proud of him. We had wonderful times together when he was in the army as a medic. I would share with him my cases. He would listen, soak it up, practice on me. His unit knew he was scheduled to become a doctor. His application already had been sent into medical school. He was two months shy of discharge when the war broke out.

We did not know until one week later that Jacob had fallen. Two men entered my office, followed by a medic. I immediately began searching through my drawers, my pocket, for Jacob's ID number, convinced it was the wrong ID, that they had the wrong soldier. And then I had to tell my wife. This was the most difficult thing I have ever had to do in my life. Ruth is a mother of Israel and this carries a great responsibility and burden. No mother should have to bear the sorrow that my wife has had to endure. Women in this country have to send their sons off to the army, to war. These are not childish games. The threat is real. There is no other country in the world like this. The second greatest difficulty was telling the grandparents. I will never forget the sound from Jacob's grandmother, a deep, deep groan.

When we came to the apartment, it was ten a.m. I had never before come home in the morning. Ruth saw the man behind me and started screaming, "Get out of here. Get out of here." She kicked them out. She had had a foreboding that something had gone terribly wrong.

We found out later that the soldiers in Jacob's unit were forbidden to talk to us, ordered to stay away from the families whose sons had fallen. When we found this out we were very angry that the army had not told us when they knew. For an entire week we lived suspended. We did not hear from Jacob. We did not hear from the army. Golda Meir later admitted that she did not disclose the statistics earlier—1,200 soldiers fell on the Golan and in the Sinai during those first two days of war—to protect the Israeli people. She did not feel the Israeli people could take it! This was a tremendous blow. Of course, the Israeli people could take it. It did not make much difference whether it was the second or the fifth day. When I was finally told, I would say it was disbelief more than anything else. I just could not comprehend it.

It was the first night, before shiva began, that I made the decision to join the army. I often find—and I do not know why—that I make decisions in the middle of the night, when things suddenly become clear to me as to what I have to do. It is my way of coping. I am an activist and this is how I respond to situations.

So the next morning I put on my army fatigue clothing that soldiers wear on inactive duty. I went to Tel Hashomer, a major hospital in Israel, that also serves as a military hospital where the army recruits come and where the medical officers are. "I want to talk to the chief of the medical service," I said. "What's up?" the man in charge asked. I explained I had just received news that my son had fallen on the Golan and I must get into the war. I added that they could use me in any capacity. I was a general practitioner, had treated intensive-care patients, performed surgery and could do anesthesia. I did not care. I wanted to get as close as possible to the front line.

I was to report the next day. I now had to tell my wife I was leaving, that I would not be there for shiva. I felt impelled. I had to be involved. My wife probably needed me more than I needed to go, but I did not think of that at the time.

As a medical officer, they assigned me to the evacuation units of the wounded from the Sinai, at the Zefim base near the canal. Though they made it very clear to me that I was not to participate in the helicopter units, I was there for several weeks and flew back and forth many times. Every time I returned to Jerusalem, I would go home. Nobody was watching or timing me since I was a volunteer. It was very meaningful to me to be a part of it.

In retrospect, I went to the front to identify with my son, to experience what he had experienced. I wanted to be in the fighting like he had been. I concluded that extraordinary events demanded extraordinary actions. This was the phrase I invented and repeated to myself many times. This was my extraordinary action.

The business of mourning was peculiar. It did not seem real. It meant so much when people came to visit, not as an obligation or ceremony, but to tell us about Jacob—things we did not know. At the time, some people could not get away from their jobs or were terribly injured, like Menachem, Jacob's commanding officer. From various people we learned new things about Jacob. This meant a great deal.

Jacob had not been living at home for two-and-a-half years. While in the army, he only came home occasionally. To us, he was still away. It was not like he was a child that had been home and now there an empty spot. We did not yet feel his daily absence. That came later.

We never directly blamed the army. It is not a question of blame. It is a Greek tragedy. In their plays, the Greeks do not blame; rather, events unfold. It is what the Gods decree. Mistakes have undoubtedly been made. But I am not terribly interested in this. It will not bring back my son. I do not blame this on anyone except the Syrians. Our rage is against the Syrians. I think of this very often. I'd like to kill them. All of them.

The first time I was shipped out, I met one of my good friends who had been called to reserve duty. His reaction showed me what can happen to some people when they are gripped by fear. When he heard Jacob had fallen he said, "I have to leave Israel. I am not going to let this happen to my son." In fact, he did leave the country a few years later. Ironically, his son insisted on returning to join the army, and he demanded that his family return with him. This sort of comment did not hurt me. It had the opposite reaction. It made me feel slightly above these people, as if they did not realize that sacrifice is sometimes required or even demanded from you.

Gideon Ginossar

Jacob and his family moved from Seattle, Washington to Israel on September 1, 1968. I was very excited to meet a new family all the way from the United States! The day felt endless in the summer heat. Television, air-conditioning and cars were scarce in Israel back then. And they drove a Mercedes! I couldn't speak with Ruth and Morty as they did not know Hebrew, but Jacob and Hava knew a few words and so we were able to communicate. We first met through our dogs. Snooky and my dog got along well, and in the beginning our relationship was based on them. In fact, two weeks after they arrived, Ruth asked if I would take care of Snooky while they vacationed in Eilat. From that moment Jacob and I were inseparable.

My father worked for the Israeli embassy as the Israeli attaché to the Common Market. In 1969, he was assigned to Belgium for three years. Until my family left, Jacob and I walked or took the bus to school together every day. One day in late spring, a large car from the Ministry arrived to take my family to the airport. Jacob was sitting at the curb waiting for me. Only a year before he had left America and now I, his best friend, was leaving him. We spoke little. As we drove away I looked back. Jacob, with his erect, confident posture, suddenly appeared frail and small like an abandoned, wounded gazelle.

Jacob's contagious enthusiasm always led to mischief. He would play all kinds of pranks on his neighbors. One neighbor was obsessed with his garden, so Jacob flooded it with water. He was a great saxophone player and the girls were crazy about him. He would share stories with me and I would listen in awe. I was his best friend. He told me everything.

Jacob adored his father, they were very close. At 16, Morty taught him how to drive his motorcycle. From this point until Jacob left for the army they shared constant adventures. Jacob wanted to be a doctor like him. I know that I am a doctor today because of Jacob. I became a medic in the army because Jacob was a medic. Before Jacob, I had never thought about medicine as a career. I hated the sight of blood. No one in my family was in this field.

During army training, soldiers walked long distances through the mountains surrounding Jerusalem. Often the soldiers bore wounds and fractures that required immediate attention. Jacob's happiness at being able to assist gave him an inner joy, and I found myself engaged by his enthusiasm. I wanted to be like him. To me, he was a symbol of the right way to live. I realize now that I ended up living Jacob's lost life.

SIMHONA WEBER

JACOB AND I FELL IN LOVE THE MOMENT WE MET. We felt so blessed to
have found each other. It was as if we were one head, one heart, one soul.
We gave all of ourselves to our love. In the two years we were together, we
never had even one argument. We did not want to be with other people.
There was so much to share, to discuss, to love. When Jacob and I were
together it was as if nothing else mattered, nothing else existed. We knew
what each other thought, what each other felt, without speaking aloud.
How many are blessed to experience even one great love in their lives?

I sit and listen and try and imagine her private thoughts:

Dear Jacob. It has been a generation since you died. I do not cry any-
more. My tears no longer flow, like the Banyas waterfalls. They stopped. I
know not when or how or even why. The first seven years were hard. Rarely
did I sleep deeply or awake refreshed. Dreams, when you appeared, were a
great comfort but also a wrenching awakening, when I would rise and have
to face the new morning. I lived in a fog and lost my inner compass, which
took years to regain. Living fills up the space for long stretches. I cope.

I remember the time we took a trip into the Negev for a weekend. Do you
remember, my love? We were so excited that we forgot to plan and did not
take enough food and water.

We lie under the stars. The cobalt sky extends into the infinite cosmos as
Ursa Major stretches across space like a glittering rope. The North Star shines
her protective beam. Now your silent heart beats no more.

The Lord will have war with Amalek
from generation to generation.

—Exodus 17:16

When you are at war in your land against
an aggressor who attacks you, you shall
sound short blasts on the trumpets, that
you may be remembered before the Lord your
God and be delivered from your enemies.

—Numbers 10:9

Chapter Three

E R E V   Y O M   K I P P U R ,   1 9 7 3

*The Lord said to Joshua "Do not be afraid
of them, for I will deliver them into your
hands; not one of them shall withstand you."*

—Joshua 10:8

Modern orthodox, a father of six children, Menachem Amsbacher is a large man, bright, intimidating, imposing. He possesses a direct manner and has a good, well-meaning heart. His size and manner instill leadership and confidence. He is quick to solve problems that need immediate attention. He accepts the dark, evil side of man and harbors few illusions. He deeply loves his country, his ideals, and these, along with his work and family, give him his purpose and direction. He takes all of them seriously and with zeal. I would call him a passionate man, in a quiet and deliberate sort of way. He does not waste time nor does he have time to waste. Handsome, with penetrating blue eyes, he could have gone far on his looks alone, but they are not important to him and he does not pay them much attention.

Menachem can break into a large, expansive smile, but he did this rarely and it always caught me off guard. I did not expect this kind of smile from him. It was a smile so warm and inviting, so beautiful and joyous, that I found myself sad when it would disappear as fleetingly as it had arrived. This smile had the feeling of magic, appearing first in front of me and then in back and then not appearing at all. I only knew that, when he gave it, he was allowing me to experience a side to him that he did not part with easily nor give away freely.

As Menachem began his story, I knew it was the last thing he desired to do. He spoke for the memory of the fallen. He felt a responsibility to tell their story and an even larger one to tell his own.

M ENACHEM A MSBACHER

N O ONE SUSPECTED WAR. In fact, the base was practically deserted because many soldiers had gone home for Yom Kippur. This turned out
to be critical. We lost much precious time mobilizing our soldiers from
active duty and the reserves. And by the time Intelligence confirmed the
war, it was too late.

As commander, I was given orders to leave our base at El Al and head
north to Tel Saki. Tel Saki was an isolated post that served for night obser-
vation to help prevent terrorism. My job was to identify the sources of any
shooting and to report any other data to my commander, Major Yaya
Yoram. I expected shooting. I took four soldiers with me.

Left: Menachem

Left to right: Benny Hanni, Itzhak Kahane, Menachem, Eliezer Agasi

Itzhak Kahane, a tall, lean man, does not skip around in his thoughts or speech. Controlled, his direct manner leaves little room for small talk or for getting acquainted. The battle of Tel Saki fundamentally changed his life. Sharing the story, instructing new recruits about its meaning, charges his life with all-consuming passion and purpose.

In all the hours I spent with him, Itzhak never smiled. He never stopped talking, repeating the facts, the minute, hour-by-hour, day-by-day details. Exhausted and drained by his exactness, precision and control, I understood that I was experiencing his intense reliving and ungluing of the event.

When I first met him I thought he was cross-eyed. Later, he shared that he had lost his eye at Tel Saki. This loss motivated him to endure a dozen eye operations and the agony of repeated operative failures. Reflective and driven, Itzhak has been unable to shake the memory of Tel Saki. His fight for the land he loves has been the greatest battle of his life.

ITZHAK KAHANE

FOR ME, THE THEME OF THE BATTLE OF TEL SAKI can best be understood around the issue of loyalty, loyalty to each other and loyalty to the IDF. We were very good soldiers and liked to help each other: if one was in danger, the other would risk his life to help him. Tragically, this came to be tested and the results were devastating.

I was responsible for 78 soldiers in a special parachute unit of Nahal. Many of the soldiers from this unit knew each other before they joined. This created a special bond between them and the officers. Most of the soldiers were like me. We had started our army service in 1970, and by October 1973 we were at the end of active duty. We had not participated in the 1967 War nor the War of Attrition at the Suez Canal. During active duty it had been quiet, so by 1973 the soldiers were eager to see some action—not war, but action. We were ordered to the Golan not to fight a war but to practice exercises. Every two months a new unit was assigned to the Syrian border. This plan had been in effect long before the war. For example, when we began our exercises in April 1973, my unit knew we would be stationed in the Golan from October until the end of November.

One of our main missions when we arrived was to patrol the border twice a day as a safeguard against terrorist activity. Other groups were assigned to specific strategic positions to guard against night terrorism. Another group was assigned to watch for any movement by Syrian military on their side of the border.

The war began Yom Kippur, October 6, at two in the afternoon. On Monday, October 2, we drove to the Golan. When we arrived, we saw many Syrian tanks, cannons and soldiers along the border. Many signs, supported by our Intelligence, told us that our enemies were mobilizing for war. Our Information told us their numbers! Nobody believed it. This insolent attitude was reflected by Prime Minister Golda Meir, Minister of Defense Moshe Dayan and the soldiers in the field. Even after the war began, we still did not believe it was war. We felt too strong. This arrogant attitude became our main problem and led to crushing consequences.

This theme of arrogance was repeated often by the soldiers who fought. Exaggerating one's own importance from an individual point of view and as a society as a whole became a fatal flaw of the war.

Right: Itzhak

SHLOMO AVITAL

WHEN WE AWOKE SATURDAY MORNING, it was cool and peaceful. Little could we anticipate that this calm would never be felt again, would always be remembered with a heavy sadness. Shabbat in the army is quiet, special. The entire Israeli army honors Shabbat. The day does not demand the same pressure and exercises.

Menachem, Eliezer, Shaya, Roni and I were ordered to Tel Saki to clear the road for land minds. I was surprised by the order but did not give it much more thought than that. Tel Saki is not a large mountain. It is only twenty to 25 meters high. The distance between the main road and Tel Saki is only a few hundred meters. The bunker itself, only three by two meters with two openings. Casually, I took my camera because photography was my hobby. I also took my pouch filled with ammunition, and hopped onto the blended car.

Left: Meir Brukenthal; second from left: Shlomo

Right: Shlomo

ELIEZER AGASI

About Jacob. IN 1973, IT WAS UNUSUAL TO MEET A BOY who had immigrated to Israel from the United States and who loved the country so much. Jacob loved Israel. He loved the army. He would stop anyone who spoke disparagingly about Israel. "We need to help our country. Israel is our country," he would say. This feeling also was evident in his parents. During shiva, his parents spoke of their love for Israel. It was beautiful to hear, considering they had just lost their son.

Jacob's confident and joyous spirit affected whatever he touched and whoever he met. His passionate nature, seen in very few, was contagious and carried one along, like a vessel travelling upon a moving stream.

Tall like his father, Jacob wanted to be a doctor as well, and this is why he became a paramedic. It was a serious decision, as the paramedic must always be at the front during war. But it was his basic nature and not his training that motivated Jacob in this direction. If one needed help, one went to Jacob.

During active duty, Jacob always searched for soldiers to pose as patients so that he could practice his newfound medical skills. There also were two paramedics training in the unit. The other soldiers did not tolerate them. Who wants to keep getting blood drawn? The other paramedics kept asking, "Why do you agree when Jacob asks and with us you decline?" No one could refuse Jacob. He drew blood without pain due to his gentle nature and beautiful smile.

The morning of Yom Kippur was very quiet. We could feel tension in the air and we thought that there might be an exchange of bombs, but this was all. We were too young to be afraid and too excited that something was actually going to happen. Our hard training had taught us to run with heavy packs, to act like soldiers when there was no war. None of us had seen action. We ran to the car when we were ordered! I thought we would finish in one or two days and then I would return to my family. It was only after the war began that this initial excitement and perception changed.

Right: Eliezer

Right: Eliezer

Left: Yair; center: Jacob

About Jacob. IN THE ARMY I WAS A PARACHUTIST. Yaya was my commander and Menachem my commanding officer. Jacob was a paramedic. I loved how Jacob spoke Hebrew with his American accent, and I often teased him.

There was one particular incident I remember with great clarity. We were on field patrol and I had a pain so severe that I felt I should report it to Menachem. I was just about to do this when Jacob appeared. He checked me out and told me that he did not think I should continue with patrol. He informed me he could not give me a pass because he did not have permission to do this. Army regulations state that only a senior paramedic can give an order to dismiss a soldier. So I went to Menachem and he asked me if I had been seen by the senior paramedic. I told him I had not but that Jacob had checked me out and felt I should not go. Remember that in the army there is a status given to the soldiers who can give an order. Jacob and I were of the same rank so he could not dismiss me from my duty. However, Menachem said that if Jacob had told me to stay, then that was good enough for him, and I should stay.

At that moment, everything changed. All the soldiers who had been standing within hearing distance suddenly felt that Jacob was no longer one of us; in our minds he had been raised to something greater. Menachem's response had elevated Jacob's status. From that moment on, Jacob had to think more seriously about his recommendations: who should be given a pass to be dismissed and who should not.

September 1973 hosted an explosion of autumn wildflowers throughout the Golan. The cool, dry air and rugged, empty terrain created a tranquil peacefulness. During the day the sun stretched across the wide, open space and created endless vistas, breathtaking points. The cold nights burned with diamond stars, with no city lights to block their beams to earth.

This tranquil beauty exploded a week before Rosh Hashana. Without warning, a state of emergency was ordered. No soldier was allowed on leave. From this moment on, until Yom Kippur, we felt only tension.

It often has been asked why were we not mobilizing—preparing ourselves for war—if we felt this tension. The foot soldiers were prepared and ready. Why were we not at the higher level? For example, the army did not order a mobilization. From our tel, only thirty kilometers from the border, we had only 25 tanks and five hundred soldiers. How different the situation would have been had we had two hundred tanks ready for attack instead of 25.

Erev Yom Kippur we were dressed in uniform, fully equipped, preparing for services. In one corner, a group of soldiers prayed. Twenty meters from them, another group ate, and further from them a group played guitars. This is how it is in the army. One group prays as another group talks, one group eats as another group plays music.

At this moment, we noticed in the valley below two shepherds with a herd of cattle that we had never seen before. This group of cattle, in this valley, at this time of day was unheard of. No one else was there. Our scouts told us to shoot at them so that they would move away. Menachem asked for permission. It was denied for fear that, coupled with the incredible tension, it could create severe consequences. Only after the war did we learn these shepherds were Syrian officers on surveillance for their army, surveying the field to determine where to fire cannons and artillery.

We finished our praying and patrolling, returned to base and waited. The war began at two in the afternoon the next day.

The Arrival at Tel Saki

The night before God makes His decision as to
who is going to live and who is going to die.

Soldiers turn toward Jerusalem for early morning prayers. *Shema Yisrael Adonoi Elohanu Adonoi Echad.* The words come forth by rote, like breath going in and out.

The meaning behind this snapshot lies in this act of prayer. Mortal soldiers, in the presence of something far greater than themselves, stand surrounded by solid, permanent rock upon harsh and barren land. Their prayers become silent protectors, humble reminders against life's cruel and random selection, and provide a comfort from the harsh reality of war.

These soldiers do not wait until war to pray. The image is about this decision. They proclaim God's force the same way in peace.

Heartfelt prayer is essential to soul as rock is fated to land. Circumstance and surrounding do not matter as these soldiers utter the ancient words and proclaim their Covenant with God.

The essential thing is the life of the individual. This alone makes history, here alone do the great transformations first take place, and the…whole history of the world, ultimately spring. In our most private and subjective lives we are not only the passive witnesses of our age, and its sufferers, but also its makers.

—C.G. Jung, *The Meaning of Psychology for Modern Man*

Chapter Four

_____

S C A T T E R E D   P I E C E S

Jacob and Simhona pause to share a private moment. His long body stretches out as he talks only for Simhona's ears. She smiles at the camera. This smile makes me conscious of the photographer who is taking the snapshot. It brings me into the image and then takes me out, as the soldier on patrol gazes into a distance that I cannot see.

The placement of the soldier on patrol, accented by his upward-pointed uzi like a microphone in the wings, and the placement of Jacob and Simhona create a triangle shape. The three different points frame the key focus—an unguarded moment of three soldiers in army service.

The soldier on patrol foreshadows a warning of things to come by the simple gesture of binoculars held in his hands.

Jacob and Simhona rest under this constant, watchful guard and surrender into their private language of love.

Stepping into Major General Yair Yoram's office, I am surprised by its order and simplicity. The Jewish flag. Red and green telephones. A few chairs. A large paper-free desk. An ashtray. Framed posters on the wall. "Yaya," as he is affectionately called, is already standing as I enter. Impatient. Reserved. Hurried. Tense. He is in no mood for casual conversation. He strikes me as a bulldog, his body framed in granite rock, a powerful, handsome presence. He initially seems like a big man, with his large, square face and full chest, but in actuality he is not. Yaya has the adoration and deep respect of his soldiers. No one ever spoke derisively about him.

Possessed of a quiet humor, which cracks through his shell, he pauses. This is unusual for a man who seems ready to spring. His guarded warmth is kept in check, given only to those whom, I suspect, he trusts. Merely by his presence, I could sense how the simple soldier must have felt safe, a little in awe, a little in fear, guarded by the confidence Yaya instills.

YAIR "YAYA" YORAM

IT IS NOW 22 YEARS SINCE THE '73 WAR. I have since fought the
Lebanon war and about 200 different operations beyond the borders of
Israel. It is very difficult for me to focus and to remember this battle....
I do remember that Menachem Amsbacher called me God. This is what
they all say. I am not religious, but do you think I am God, that God sent
me to save? My responsibility as battalion commander stretched from the
middle to the south of the Golan Heights. At the time war broke, I was
studying near Tel-Aviv. I immediately left and took over this battalion.
I had been familiar with it for years.

Avigdor Kahalani, a compact, charismatic man, greets me warmly. Full of generous, earthy enthusiasm, he instills confidence and natural leadership. He puts me at ease immediately, and I feel as if I have known him for a long time. He exudes energy and dynamism, and is poised to take on the world, bold and assured that no problem is too small or too complex. Intuitively sharp, politically astute, ambitious, Kahalani showed a deep understanding of human nature and an openness and reflection into himself.

Top left: Avigdor

AVIGDOR KAHALANI

IN THE SIX DAY WAR we were in the offensive position. We attacked and surprised them. We invented our own way of defeating them by our artillery, aircraft, bombs and soldiers. During the Yom Kippur War, it was entirely different. We had to react. This put us at a big disadvantage. We knew the facts, saw their tanks move to the border, but we thought it was a training exercise. We were surprised to see how much courage they had, to start a war in the middle of the day, but also by how much courage we had, too.

I was not in the area of Tel Saki. I was a battalion commander of the tanks. Yaya was the battalion commander of the paratroops. The Golan Heights was divided into two parts, the north and the south. My area was the north, the 7th Armored Brigade. The southern area was the 188th Armored Brigade. Yaya was in charge of the southern brigade. Only after the war did I become brigade commander and division commander of the entire Golan Heights.

The Yom Kippur War was a shock. We lost nearly three thousand lives. As a tough commander, I demanded that my soldiers do all they could to protect the country, the area, themselves. This war was much more difficult than the 1967 War. After the 1967 War, I was in the hospital for a year. I had 16 operations. Sixty percent of my body had been burned. Now I had to fight again. I did not know if I could get back inside a tank. I feared I had something terrible inside, like a permanent trauma.

I do remember everything very clearly...
We were the eyes...the only way the IDF
knew what was going on.

—Menachem Amsbacher

Chapter Five

THE WAR BEGINS

MENACHEM

DURING WAR, it is important to be familiar with the topography of the region. In the northern part of the Golan, there are many mountains. The southern part, instead of mountains, has a large valley, the Jordan River and many elevations or tels (small hills.) In the Yom Kippur War, the largest concentration of soldiers was in the south. We were stationed in this area.

Tel Saki is two kilometers from the Syrian border, 13 kilometers from El Al. From Tel Saki one can see across the border, assess and process information. Tel Saki was actually two small hills with a large, flat valley that was impossible to cross without being seen. Nearby, a deep canyon created a natural border between Syria and Israel. A small alley in the corner led to the main road. This road led directly to the settlements and Tiberias. Tel Saki was the highest point at this junction.

The bunker was built toward the center of the hill. A cube shape with two openings, one on each side. Tel Saki was not prepared for war. It was not protected and not built underground. There were no land mines around it, and in the ammunition boxes we found stones instead of ammunition.

I positioned our soldiers at different locations and placed myself and Shlomo at the entrances. We were only five soldiers with our weapons. We had no other men to help if the Syrians attacked. There was little to do when we arrived, so we rehearsed strategy. I suspected the Syrian army was trying to penetrate Israel. I also knew that once it became dark we would not be able to see because we did not have any night vision equipment. By listening to communication I learned that many Syrian troops were around, but I did not know where.

Noise. It seemed to come from a convoy from the north. It was headed toward us. I used the heavy machine gun attached to the blended car and aimed toward the main road. We hit one Syrian tank. It burst into flames. I verified with my troops that no one was moving our forces, so I knew this one had to be Syrian. I had seen them trying to penetrate through the northern part and suspected they were trying to move south toward Tiberias, the heart of Israel.

I shot again. I hit another one. I quickly saw a Syrian convoy so large that I could not see the end. It was out of range from my machine gun. I did not know if I had hit the tank from the beginning, the middle or the end of the convoy. All I knew was that the convoy was continuing south. We hit many tanks but the Syrians simply crawled out of them and took position behind rocks.

I reported to my base that I feared some Syrian tanks may have passed me and were riding toward El Al, and that a battalion of tanks was approaching from the north. We suddenly became afraid. We knew the Syrians would not fear our infantry. One feels hermetically sealed and relatively safe inside a tank. Another soldier looked through the binoculars and said on the communication system, "Your officer does not understand the scales and armor in tanks. This is not a battalion but a brigade!" One hundred and fifty tanks, or one thousand Syrian soldiers! There were no other Israeli soldiers between us five paratroopers at Tel Saki, the El Al base camp where Yaya stood, or the 45-minute ride to Tiberias.

ITZHAK

THE SITUATION WAS GRAVE BY FRIDAY AFTERNOON, Erev Yom Kippur.
I received orders that all soldiers were to remain at the base. The others on
leave were to return immediately. High Alert. Nobody spoke of war. We
suspected bombing, a skirmish, maybe an attempt to cross the border, but
that was all. This was why I ordered Menachem to take a group of soldiers
and go to Tel Saki. I had no idea that when Menachem left I would not see
him again until the end of the war. From that moment on our only contact was by radio.

Benny Hanni and I were the two officers in charge. Major Yaya Yoram
did not arrive at El Al until late Saturday afternoon. He was a superb officer who inspired confidence and was well-liked. When he heard on the
radio that war had broken out, he immediately left his army course in
Tel-Aviv and took command of his troops. Unfortunately, his units were
separated. My unit was in El Al. Some soldiers were with Menachem at
Tel Saki. A third unit, elsewhere.

We were completely taken off guard. I had never heard a bomb before.
The ground shook like an earthquake. Everyone was astonished but there
was no panic. We were well-trained to know what to do. We still could not
believe it was war. We did not have radio and were forced to use the
radios from the tanks. It was then, when we heard the war announced
on the radio, that we knew the war had begun. I spoke with Menachem.
They too had been bombed.

We won the 1967 War by a surprise attack against the Egyptian and
Syrian air forces. This occurred during the first three hours of the war.
Now we had lost this element of surprise, and the situation quickly disintegrated. Completely unprepared psychologically, and ill-equipped, we
had too few soldiers and tanks on alert. In one moment our tank was
destroyed, another tank ran out of ammunition, a third tank had no fuel.
By evening, Menachem reported hundreds, soon thousands of Syrian
troops penetrating the border. From Saturday evening until late Monday
afternoon, when the first reserves arrived in the Golan, the situation
remained critical. The Syrians arrived in El Al during this time. We were
lucky because they could have captured Tiberias. We had too few soldiers
to defend it.

Left: Roni; center, Yair

The sounds of conversation and commotion fill this action-packed snapshot. Roni's exhaustion can be easily read by his body language, which is in sharp contrast to his usual humor and teasing. Yair gives him his total attention, oblivious to the chaos around them. He holds his uzi as straight as he carries his posture erect. Amid the sounds of loud voices, the two remain engrossed.

The image—filled with boots, backs of heads, soldiers moving in various directions, army gear, guns and aluminum barracks—becomes a statement of the transitory moments of army life.

The urgent situation can be felt by the fact that the photographer has been ignored. Only the soldier behind Yair acknowledges his presence. An imperceptible triangle, formed by these three soldiers, compasses this frozen present. Roni speaks in the moment, Yair responds from the moment, and the soldier with glasses looks beyond the moment.

How often do our lives brush up against another's without our knowing that this may be our last meeting, our last conversation? A week later Roni will be dead and Yair barely alive. What is taken as a casual and insignificant encounter, recorded by an amateur photographer, becomes a treasured and permanent recording of last words.

SHLOMO

"THE SYRIANS ARE ONLY TESTING THEIR MISSILES," we are told. "It is just another test." We know it is more. We are at Tel Saki and there are only five of us. The situation is out of control, dangerous. Hundreds are crossing the border. We offer no resistance. They must be shocked, I think to myself.

The direct missile. The hole. It wounds Shaya, myself and others. I do not feel my wounds. I do not realize how badly I am hurt. They continue to attack. We try to shoot back. Menachem is the first to fall. He is hit in the legs. Roni, my best friend, is working the machine gun. He is killed instantly by a stray bullet. The situation is hopeless. None of us have any protection.

It is now my turn to use the machine gun that Roni was using when he was killed. I see their bullets fly over my head because the direction of the bullet can be seen by its red tail. It is at this moment that an intuitive awareness, like a profound, clear click, seizes me. I suddenly know that I will live. I have no explanation for this immediate truth, but I know that someone is protecting me. I do not know how long this feeling lasts; it feels like hours but it is probably shorter than a second. I trust in this still clarity with all my heart.

The first night at Tel Saki I have a dream. In the dream I am sitting inside the bunker. It is cold and somber, an overwhelming sadness invades the dark. All my friends are crying. Roni, he is crying hardest of all. I am present but no one can see me. I watch with them as my body drops into the newly unearthed grave. Dirt is shoveled upon my rigid, wrapped form. No one speaks. Muffled sounds of tears can be heard. Except for Roni. He sobs openly, without shame. And then my present life unfolds, like watercolor. There is no escape from where we are, this isolated, bare army post where so few have travelled. Then my life switches again and I watch, in flashback, the life of my past. Abba. Imma. Oh Abba. Don't leave me now. You are my strength, the voice that calms. And then I suddenly wake up. I look around. Unidentified night sounds put fear into my soul. I remember my dream. To this day, I do not know why this dream gave me the conclusion that it did. But I know after this dream I will live.

According to the psychology of Carl G. Jung, dreams are the language that God uses to communicate. Dreams are images and symbols of the unconscious. If Jung could have interpreted this dream, he might have told Shlomo that he was afraid to see his own death. The dream provided this experience. The unconscious made it possible for Shlomo to experience the reality of his own death. In the dream, Shlomo watches the process of his death, an experience during war too horrible for him to accept otherwise. The dream gave him a larger perspective of the war and a greater insight into himself. The unconscious had completed the picture of death and his psyche had survived.

Like Joseph in the Bible, Shlomo did not understand the meaning of his dream at the time. He only knew that it possessed a numinous quality. This could be seen in the impact it still had on him so many years later. Shlomo's dream gave him great strength and later allowed him to perform heroic acts.

There is a lapse of time from when a missile is discharged to when it explodes. A soldier can see its route in the sky by the color trail it leaves. In those moments, a world passes by, prayers are mailed.

The black volcanic pyramid rock dominates this image. Pausing, the unseen soldier hides, positioned against the enduring rock, watching from afar the powerful missile.

The Babylonians, Greeks, Assyrians, Romans, Crusaders, Turks, British and Jordanians have tried to control this five-thousand-year-old land and stone. But faith is stronger than man's ability to dominate. Against God's majestic power, this soldier takes a moment to wait in this solitary landscape, this war zone, before he continues onward.

Eliezer

The Syrian direct attack begins early Sunday morning and lasts six hours. We are only five soldiers but fight as if we were many. We convince the Syrians of this because they decide to stay and battle us, a critical fight that preoccupies them for many important hours. Why bother if there are only five soldiers? It is a miracle they do not leave and move directly into Israel. They can conquer all the land. There is nothing else to stop them.

We have only one blended car that has an attached machine gun. The Syrians are unrelenting in trying to explode our car. Roni fiercely uses this gun. And then he is killed. High-spirited, funny Roni. Crushed. Just like that. A passionate meteorite snuffed out, like a candle flame against a sudden gust of air. A hushed silence grips us. The pounding gunfire continues. Menachem moves into Roni's vacant space until he is badly hit. Now it is my turn. I cannot allow myself to feel or to think. As a trained soldier, I automatically do my job and use this gun until I run out of ammunition and Syrian bodies are strewn around. Only then do we retreat into the bunker.

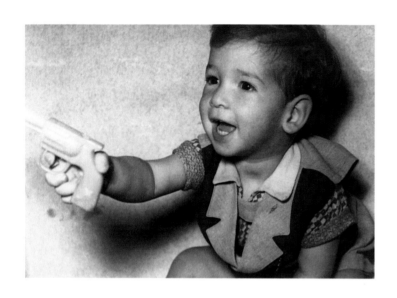

HANNA ELIRAZ

RONI ENTERED THE ARMY IN 1971 and was nearly finished with his active service when the war broke out. My mother and I lived in constant fear because we did not hear from him. He was the firstborn. I was 13 years old at the time. Our father died when Roni was ten. He was only a child, but the moment our father died Roni took the responsibilities upon himself and became the man in the family. He protected me. I idolized him. When Roni died, my family filled with a permanent sadness. It was never the same again. There was no more laughter.

Three days before Roni died, Shlomo took this photograph. Roni's laughter and radiant spirit changed the energy in any room. Every soldier interviewed spoke of him. He was responsible and mature, full of contagious life. This young boy's beautiful and rare spirit leaps out of the frame, as he leapt out of life.

Rocks fill this barren landscape. The parched land is home to them. Worn paths disappear and then reappear several yards later. Undercurrents of air pick up sand particles and carry them into the war. From the naked eye, nothing has changed. The same rocks. The same terrain for thousands of years.

Yet, in front, filling almost half the frame, is Roni. Soon, his flame will be extinguished. He will burn into a million lights, as his spirit, pumped out of his body, disappears into the harsh sun, only to return in the brilliant stars that radiate the blackest night.

One needs to believe in something for which
one can have whole-hearted enthusiasm.
One needs to feel that one's life has meaning,
that one is needed in this world.

—Hannah Senesh, *Her Life and Diary*

When I made aliyah to this country, I was reborn.

—Jacob Rayman

Chapter Six

THE WAR ESCALATES

Center: Jacob

MENACHEM

YAYA ORDERS TWO ARMORED CARRIERS TO THE BORDER of one of the
sparse settlements located between Tel Saki and the army base. The
plan is to wait in ambush and surprise the Syrians, put fear into them.
Commander of the first vehicle is Benny Hanni and commander of the
second is Ariel Weitzman. Jacob sits in the second armored carrier. They
arrive in time and wait. Just before sunrise, two armored Syrian carriers
appear and are hit from less than fifty meters. In ambush it is critical
that there are no mistakes. Our soldiers are hit at least once. In hindsight,
they should have turned back and returned to El Al. The area was Syrian-
controlled. Instead, our soldiers wait. When day breaks they are given
their next orders.

ITZHAK

OUR SITUATION BECAME DESPERATE as hundreds of Syrians kept crossing over Saturday night. They did not go directly to Tel Saki; instead, they continued south toward El Al and tried to pass. They shot and bombed Tel Saki. By night the Syrians had successfully penetrated. A dark terror crept into our souls.

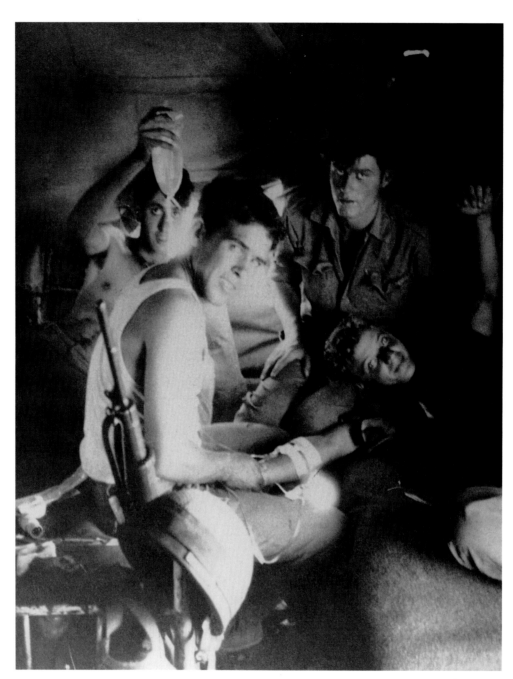

Upper right: Jacob

YAIR

BY SATURDAY NIGHT, we were in defensive positions around the base. I heard that Menachem and a small group had gone to Tel Saki and needed support. One of the armored carriers used for the rescue mission needed another man. I volunteered. In this small carrier, I reconnected with my friends. We were told there were no more Israeli tanks between Tel Saki and the settlement Ramat Magshimim, and that the only remaining tanks were Syrian. We waited in ambush as many bombs exploded around us. I found myself next to Jacob. He was very quiet. "Don't worry," I said to him. "If anything happens call out for me and I will protect you." I do not know what made me say this or why. What made me think I could protect him? We sensed the gravity. Our hearts spoke the truth. These words, these haunting, beautiful words later would come back to torment me. There is no agony like failing yourself and your dearest friend. Jacob turned and looked into my face. His dark eyes possessed an overwhelming sadness that penetrated right though me. He said nothing. It was as if he knew his fate. This was the last picture of Jacob that I remember, those deep, still, sad eyes.

All night we lay in wait until the bare morning light. We felt fortunate that we survived. Every passing carrier traveling from Tel Saki was Syrian. There were no Israeli tanks. Suddenly, through a torrent of dust, we saw a tank directly heading toward us. We quickly aimed to shoot when we realized it was Israeli. This tank was one of the remaining few that functioned. In actuality, it was missing its large cannon in front, did not have any bombs, and was full of wounded soldiers. They were from a different unit and were desperately trying to refuel and reload, after surviving a brutal attack from the Syrians. Little did I know at the time that one of the men in this tank would play a critical role in my life.

Three soldiers pause, exhausted, too tired to speak. Soldiering is hard. Stressful. Heavy packs. Weapons. Primitive conditions. Tight quarters. No soft beds. No hot showers. No home cooking.

Jacob sits in quiet introspection, his large, handsome, sculpted face taking over a third of the image. One soldier looks far into the distance. Another soldier bends his head in fatigue. This image speaks of the time between, from having left to going toward, from having seen to turning back. They journey in the vessel that carries them to their destination.

I am reminded of a story Jacob's father once told. A friend of his shared a conversation that he had with Jacob a month before he fell:

Jacob and I were talking and I said to him, "Look at you, Jacob. You are exhausted. You are dirty and tired. You have been through all this army business. If you had stayed in America, you'd be having a wonderful time now. You'd be going out on dates and to parties and fraternities and football games and everything. Instead, you are risking your life. What do you think about this?" Jacob answered in Hebrew, "When I made aliyah to this country, I was reborn."

MENACHEM

Just before sunrise, when there is enough light, the Syrians head south towards us. The battle begins. We fight until noon. Fortunately for us the Syrians do not know we are only five soldiers. If they had, they would have easily overwhelmed us and marched directly into Israel. It is silly to fight such a big battle against only five soldiers. They attack us with rockets, in tanks and on their bellies. We make many efforts to pretend we are many. We shoot from one rock and then we crawl to another rock on the other side and shoot behind this rock. We do this to make them believe there are two soldiers instead of one.

Soon all the territory is occupied by them. They establish a base and have a very strong position from which to shoot. We are surrounded. I try to get permission to leave the outpost but the IDF is relying heavily on our reports. It is impossible to fight one thousand Syrians with five soldiers. There are more soldiers than cartridges in our guns! However, the IDF has too many reports that Syrians are everywhere; they need to get a precise picture of the battle in order to send the reserves to the right place. The IDF cannot get a clear picture from the air, either. It is all missile-threatened, meaning our air force cannot fly in the skies to obtain a precise picture of the war below. We are ordered to stay and delay the Syrians as much as we can. By the time permission to withdraw comes, it is too late.

ITZHAK

WHEN WE FINALLY GAVE THE ORDER TO MENACHEM TO LEAVE, it was too late. Their blended car had been destroyed during the Saturday bombing, Menachem was too badly hurt to return on his own, and most of his soldiers were seriously wounded. Menachem was crying for help.

Early Sunday morning we gave the order to rescue them. My last officer, Benny Hanni, was ordered to go. He took with him two armored carriers filled with soldiers, arrived at their destination near Ramat Magshimim, and stayed the night waiting in ambush. However, Syrian tanks had passed Tel Saki and were waiting in ambush as well.

Confusion. "We are jumping! We are jumping! The Syrians are shooting. We are jumping!" Benny yells over the radio. Although I did not realize it at the time, this was the last time I would hear his voice. Sunday morning, Menachem realizes he is completely surrounded. Meir Brukenthal and I rush to our car. What has happened? Privately we are frantic inside, although outwardly we remain in control. We must try and rescue our soldiers. What has happened to them?

From my pent prison I put forth my head
And call unto the storm and question it,
And search the clouds and with the gloom confer—
When will the darkness and the tempest pass?
When will the whirlwind die and the clouds scatter
And moon and stars break forth again in light?
I search from heaven to earth, from earth to heaven:
No sign nor answer—only storm and night.

—Hayyim Nahman Bialik, *Night*

Chapter Seven

THE LAND OF THE DEAD

Yair

POSITIONED AND READY, Syrian tanks waited for us as we arrived near Tel Saki. Jacob sat by my side. A tel blocked our view, putting us at a disadvantage because we could not see all their tanks. When our first carrier reached the top of the tel, where the sites of the northern side could be seen, it was immediately hit by a Syrian cannon. Ordered to leave the main road, we tried to reach Tel Saki from a different direction. The Syrians struck again. Our driver died instantly. We jumped from the vehicle, hid behind some rocks near the side of the road and began shooting. Soon, I noticed it became too quiet. Something felt wrong. I kept on shooting. A Syrian hiding behind a large rock saw me and shot. His bullet grazed the rock, bounced off and penetrated my neck. My rifle jammed. Bleeding profusely, blood spilling all over my gun, dizzy, I knew I was in trouble. Until I was hit, I did not feel fear, but from the moment my rifle jammed, I knew only terror. I put my hand to my neck and saw that I was losing a great deal of blood. I tried to bandage myself. I heard noise, more shooting. I threw some hand grenades. I was hit every place on my body where I was not wearing a vest or helmet.

Convinced everyone was dead, the Syrians casually wandered among our lifeless soldiers. I pretended to be dead. A Syrian walked over, took my head in his hands and moved it around. I hardly breathed. He poked me with his gun and then he left. I did not move. Parched, I feared my guard would come down if I fell asleep. What gave me the power not to pass out came from an experience I had a month before the war.

I was attending a military funeral of a commanding officer who had died in an army helicopter accident. The slain soldier's mother fainted just as they finished the traditional gun salutes. "How would my mother feel if I died?" I wondered. I forced myself not to lose consciousness. However, I must have fallen asleep because when I awoke the sun was directly above me.

YAYA

TEL SAKI. We did not change its Arabic name after we captured it. Today, Tel Saki, fortified by many underground bunkers, looks completely different. In 1973, Tel Saki consisted of two tiny bunkers set down on top of a little rocky hill, like fragile bird nests perched in a barren tree. For me, Tel Saki was not the worst battle. I was three miles south. During the Six Day War, I nearly died. I have seen other operations and wars. I have wondered from time to time if I made the right decision, but this is all. I sleep very well.

I want to ask about this decision. Is he referring to the decision that gave permission for Benny to go on the rescue mission, or the decision not to give Menachem permission to leave Tel Saki? What would he have done differently? He is telling me his story the way he wants me to hear it. There is no room for questions, answers or discussion.

Difficult for us to understand is why the Syrians stopped at Tel Saki rather than continue onward. Only a few of our soldiers were there who, with their bare hands, attempted to stop them. On their own, the Syrians stopped and waited. They did not retreat or move forward. This critical decision cost them heavily. If they had been more aggressive, they could have penetrated Israel and reached Tiberias and the entire Jordan Valley. The Syrians were very successful in the first two days of the war.

According to their doctrine, the first brigade was ordered to reach this point. The armored brigade would change places and advance. This was their plan. In spite of the fact that there was no reason to stop, they did. This is a grave mistake in war. One should not act according to the plan but according to the situation unfolding in the arena.

Standing alone, watching the Syrians through my binoculars, bare-handed, with nearly one thousand tanks facing me, I could not understand why they halted. Maybe they saw me, and because of this they would not dare come forward.

While he initially was unable to recall the battle, he now recalls the smallest details.

Nearly thirty soldiers lost their lives at Tel Saki. Not all of them were from my battalion. Sunday night, a few soldiers from my battalion and from the armored units hiding near the second bunker escaped. The Syrians never found them in spite of the fact that they were on the same little hill. I think a dozen or more were killed from another platoon, trying to reach the battalion to rescue Amsbacher's people.

Dawn. Sunday morning our soldiers battled the Syrian armored brigade. We were three blended cars against a thousand Syrians. We did not stand a chance.

He stops. His drawn face does not reveal his private thoughts. His eyes are cast downward. I notice the room has become quiet. I hear a telephone ringing in the secretarial office beyond the closed door. He looks up at me, staring, his thoughts elsewhere. I wonder what images have suddenly appeared in front of him. I wonder what he is remembering. I wonder what he will keep buried inside his heart.

R I V K A H   B E N   A H R O N

IN ISRAEL, WHEN A SOLDIER DIES his family sits shiva, a period of mourning that lasts for seven days. Friends visit to pay their respects. Yaya was afraid to make this condolence call because he was the one who had given Benny the permission to go. He did not know the reaction of my family. He knocked on the door. My father answered. Yaya broke down and cried like a baby, cried like a baby.

"Forgive me. Forgive me," he wept.

And my father asked, "For what?"

"Because I gave him the permission to go. I sent him."

"But he wanted to go," my father said.

They became good friends and spoke frequently. Yaya would often visit with my father, once telling him that when he saw Benny's eyes, he knew he had to let him go, that his eyes were burning. After he gave the permission he ran after them, warning that it was a suicide mission. Surrounded by one thousand Syrians, they went in spite of this warning because of the persistence and determination of my brother. Yaya gave the order against his own judgement, against everything he felt.

Years later, Yaya's daughter was killed in an army accident, an airplane maneuver. I wrote to him and he responded that when his daughter died, he remembered my father's words.

He added that it was only after something happened to him, when he lost his own daughter, that he felt what grieving families feel, that he really understood.

MENACHEM

THE SYRIANS KEEP TRYING TO TAKE TEL SAKI. We fight hard but most
of our ammunition is finished. Shaya Levy has an injury in his head and
lies dying. Only a few functioning soldiers remain. Like refugees, tank
soldiers from different units straggle toward and join us because Tel Saki
is the only Israeli territory left in this area. They join our desperate battle.
I report to Yaya that we can withstand one or two more hours without
reinforcements. Our ammunition has run out, our blended car has been
hit and the bazooka missile does not work. I ask for permission to abandon the outpost but cannot get it. He orders two armored carriers for a
double mission. First, to rescue us. Second, if they do not succeed, to
deliver more ammunition and soldiers.

Two armored carriers set out. We have bad communication. I warn
them not to use the main road, and that they must try and remain hidden. They arrive on the main road, see what I describe, decide to take a
different path, and stumble upon a ditch they cannot cross. This forces
them to return to the main road. We start firing at the Syrians to distract
them from our vehicles. The drivers put the carriers into full throttle and
break through hundreds of Syrians. Military rules demand space between
two vehicles because if a shell misses the first vehicle it will then hit the
second. The first carrier arrives very close to our outpost when suddenly it
is badly hit. The driver dies. No one survives. The second carrier follows
nine hundred feet behind. The driver sees what happens to the first car
but there is nothing he can do. As soon as he arrives near the outpost, his
car is hit, too.

The soldiers jump from the burning vehicle. As they touch ground
they are shot by waiting Syrians. Intense shooting breaks out for 25 minutes, heavy firing from both sides. In time only Syrian fire can be heard.
Nineteen Israeli soldiers die in this battle. Everyone is silenced by the
bravery of our soldiers. A terrible, futile sadness washes over me. The
realization that we may lose the war and that Israel could be destroyed
takes root and cruelly plants itself, like poison tentacles, inside me.

I lose track of time. I do not bother to look at my watch. I have found that when soldiers remember a battle, it is the time of events that differs in their memory. We hold on until early afternoon but we lose. The Syrians capture Tel Saki. All our ammunition is gone. I order the remaining soldiers to enter the dark bunker. There are only two iron-framed bunks without mattresses. In a formal act, I say goodby. We spoil the machine gun so the enemy cannot use it, destroy final papers, and prepare farewells to our families.

The Syrians keep shooting into the bunker. The bullets hit the wall, start ricocheting and hit my head. They throw in some grenades and succeed in killing a few more of us. The soldier behind me dies. Another grenade explodes. Immediately the bunker fills with smoke and dust. Its loud noise explodes our ear drums. The Syrians continue shooting. More noise. More grenades. You killed us, I think to myself. Enough. Take the bunker. You deserve it. Enough. Dazed. The splinters from the grenade pierce my back. Grenades keep exploding. I shout, "Anyone in the bunker who is alive, go out and surrender. Say everyone is dead." I pull my High Holiday siddur and read from the Chapter of Praises. From David, "The song from the depths we call up to thee God." I say it in a kind of a whisper but everyone can hear. A soldier leaves, waving his white t-shirt. I hear shooting. Then all is quiet.

I am told later the Syrian soldiers admire the way our soldiers fight. They do not touch the bodies as they usually do. Instead, they take the red boots from our dead soldiers as their trophy because these red boots reflect the paratroopers, an elite force of the IDF.

It is hard to imagine it was here that the spoils of war were deposited in the not-so-distant past, where bedouins squatted and shepherds roamed upon this parched and barren soil. It is hard to conceive of red blood flowing as thickly as moving streams, or of bodies lying strewn across this battlefield. As the timeless and eternal breeze flutters through the delicate eucalyptus leaves, it is hard to remember smoke so thick that days like this appeared gray.

ITZHAK

THERE IS NO TIME TO THINK. I know something terrible has happened to Benny. I take a blended car and ten soldiers to rescue the soldiers who have gone to rescue Amsbacher and his group. A rescue of the rescue. We need to regain the region.

Sunday morning. The sun rises early as we creep slowly to Tel Saki. None of us know the area. I have been there only once. As we approach the battlefield, enveloped in dust and smoke, it becomes difficult to see. A few hundred meters ahead, I see Benny's armored carrier. A sinking terror slowly creeps into me. But I still do not realize the full impact of what I am seeing. I cannot confirm if anyone is alive.

We decide not to continue on the main road and begin to travel in a different direction, when suddenly we are faced with the confrontation of another battle, and return to the main road. We reach the location of our two other carriers, jump to the ground and prepare to fight. The Syrians are waiting, and surround us on all sides.

In an instant, our driver and four of my soldiers die. Meir seizes the driver's seat to try and turn the car around, but the car is destroyed and begins to burn. I start to run with some others. The Syrians are at our heels. They never stop shooting. Four of us succeed in reaching Tel Saki. We do not enter the bunker. The Syrians are shooting inside. We avoid the smaller bunker, too. Its purpose is to hold supplies, but it stands empty and offers no protection. Instead we wait in terror, fearful they will discover us on a side of the tel. We lay only a few meters from where they are standing. All Sunday we hide, shielded by the rocks.

Chain-smoking and intense, Meir Brukenthal appears in constant motion even as he sits concentrating. Whether he is talking nonstop on his portable telephone, or being interrupted by one of his six young children, or managing one of the largest egg hatcheries in Israel, Meir remains in a state of high alert. He has the bearing of a man with the responsibility of a colonel in the IDF Reserves. All of these distractions, however, did not stop him from giving me his complete, undivided attention. His memory is as sharp as a paper cutter. Quiet, soft spoken and gentle, he is introspective, reflective and shows a heartfelt sensitivity.

MEIR BRUKENTHAL

WE HEAR BENNY SCREAMING FOR HELP and the shooting by the Syrians
over the radio. Itzhak and I gather a few soldiers into our blended car and
race to Tel Saki. We are in great fear because we do not know what has
happened to Benny. We suspect the worst. As we approach Tel Saki, we are
attacked, many of us die, and our vehicle is destroyed. Four of us run to
the bunker with bullets whizzing around our heads and backs. We do not
go in because close to the rear of the bunker is a Syrian tank filled with
soldiers. Itzhak has been hit and is badly wounded, and another soldier
has a broken leg. We huddle nearby. We hear one of our soldiers from
outside the bunker crying, "We are all dead!" Then shouting. Shooting.
Silence. We decide to bury the papers we carry. We had left the base so
quickly that we had taken information with us into battle. What if we
were captured? Hiding behind the tel, we wait in fear. We have had no
communication with Menachem and do not know if he is still alive.
All around lie our dead soldiers.

It is impossible to be in Israel and not touch stone. It is under your feet as you walk, in the dust as you breathe, on the grave when you die. It is remarkable how often stone is mentioned in the Bible. Jacob places a large stone under his head as he lies on his back. From this connection, his dream appears and the course of history is changed. He uses a stone to impress Rachel at the well. Moses and Aaron walk on lapis, the stone of the earth and sky. The Ten Commandments are written in stone. David kills Goliath with five stones. Jerusalem has more bloodshed on its stone face than any other city. Stone is the symbol of God's protective strength. It embodies divine nature.

Uneven and raw, rock is the broken face of earth. As a cover, stone protects; as a road, it supports; as a barrier, it holds; and on the grave it knocks to let the spirit in.

The infinity of the cosmos, the chaos of meaning and meaninglessness…were trapped in stone. This contained and at the same time was the…embodiment of spirit. What I felt to be my kinship with stone was the divine nature in both, in the dead and the living matter.

—C.G. Jung, *On Synchronicity*

A candle flickering in light
Gasping for air
In a final attempt to live,
Slowly slips from blossoming bright
As a Hand reaches down
And silently extinguishes the flame.

—Yael Lerman

Chapter Eight

D E A T H

PINCHAS BERKOVITCH

BLACK VOLCANIC ROCK SCARS THE TEL SAKI LANDSCAPE in which, on
Monday morning, I find Jacob's body. Jacket-cool, my army coat lies open
as I think to myself, "I should zip it closed." Not a single cloud lingers in
the pale blue sky. I remember thinking how quiet it is; only the sounds of
helicopters somewhere in the distance mar the otherwise perfect stillness.
No one talks. The radio communication chatter continues but no one
pays much attention. It seems too quiet. I remember thinking, "How
strange that I can hear wild field sparrows chirping." A large bird circles in
the sky. My feelings remain numb. You have to turn them off at times like
these. Wall them away. Otherwise it is too dangerous, too hard. You hope
it will always be like this, that this walled-off feeling will protect you from
what you see. But you are only fooling yourself. All this stuff turns into
memories later on. Hard memories. Memories that wake you up when
you sleep, that are attached to you, like your shadow in the late afternoon.

The filtered smell of death travels differently in the Golan. Mixed with
the crisp, clean air and beautiful wildflowers, death's harsh presence
appears kind. No other place on earth connects fragrances with the land
as in Israel. Something special lies here. The harshness of Israel. The
Israeli earth echoes history in Her dirt. Wild earth. Broken earth. Filled
with casualties from past conflicts and wars, this history has made the soil
rich. The fragrance of Israel. Nostalgic scents journey through time. Her
sweet, gentle perfumes catch memories in the air. Melancholy, silent
words coast through fresh Golan winds. These fragrances flutter like eye-
lash kisses against baby cheeks, quake you from the past, bring you into
the present. The smells help me find my way home. All of this is on my
mind as we approach Tel Saki. We stop the car and step out. Soldiers lie
everywhere. We have entered a killing field. Instinctively, we move in different directions to begin our clean-up. The Syrians have not mutilated
the bodies, to our great relief. Thank God for small blessings like these.
We are like drone bees, automatons, ordered to get the job done. Thinking
is too dangerous.

You hope you will not come across someone you know. Finding some-one you know unlocks you. Most of the soldiers are from other units. I pray that my luck will not run out. But it does. I find Jacob's body. He faces Tel Saki. They had come so close but failed in their rescue mission. Jacob looks so peaceful. He almost seems asleep. His face is clean, his body untouched. The only wound is directly to his chest. But this is enough. I kneel down beside him. I cannot move. I caress his face, his cheeks, with my hand. I pick him up gently, carry him to the truck. I do not want to leave him alone. I cover him with a blanket so that he will not be cold. "Why Jacob?" I ask myself. "Of all people, why Jacob?"

We finish cleaning the area. It has been the most difficult chore of my life. I survive. Jacob dies. Why? There are no answers. For a long time, long after the war, this question torments me. Jacob's brilliant light extin-guished. A touch with humanity lost.

Imagine the Bible without Jacob.

SIMHONA

I RECEIVED A LETTER FROM JACOB EVERY DAY for a week after he died. The mail takes four or five days from the army because it goes through censorship. I only became suspicious when there was no telephone call. I knew he would do anything he could to call me. I was hoping against hope. Pinchas, the soldier who found Jacob's body, called Monday night but did not tell me. He was forbidden to until Morty and Ruth had been notified. None of us found out until the following Sunday.

I was on the kibbutz when the war began, and heard that they were mobilizing soldiers. Working outdoors with a friend of mine, I found myself talking constantly about Jacob, how we were going to have lots of children because Jacob wanted ten children, how Jacob loved biology, nature, the flowers and birds of the Golan Heights. At that time, the Golan was wild and unsettled. Once we found a special flower, an iris by a sign that advertised a nature reserve. Jacob removed the sign. He did not want anyone to know about this special place. We made it ours. I kept talking, wondering why I was, seeing these ordinary moments suddenly taking on such an acute sharpness and urgency. Little did I know at the time that I would become a biologist, that when I had my first daughter I would call her Iris, that all my daughters would be named after flowers. Little did I know that, as I stood in the hot, glaring sun, unable to stop talking, trying to control a vague foreboding that my destiny already had been intersected, saddened, permanently altered by an explosion not so far away, on an unnamed, unknown, rocky mountain road.

After listening to Simhona, I imagine her experience the following way:
Mid-morning, around ten. I pause from work. Tired from my nervous chatter. My friend isn't listening. I am talking out loud to myself. Standing. Leaning. What am I leaning against? Don't remember. Momentarily blinded by a glare of sunlight that reflects upon a metal object behind me. What is it? Did something break and this was one of the pieces that was not picked up? Should turn around. Too tired. Why am I so tired? I just had breakfast not long ago. Raise my right hand to shield my eyes. What am I trying to see?

Brush a bug away with my left hand, like a thought that does not want to be known. Waving backwards with that automatic, mindless action. Wrist raised, moving back and forth, in seesaw motion with the elbow, when I focus, see from far away a delegation from the kibbutz walking toward me. They seem to move in snail-like motion, as this crushing sensation suddenly descends upon me, like a dynamited, heavy stone wall slowly collapsing. I know what they are coming to tell me. I just know. I probably have known all along, before they did. Before anyone did.

I return to Simhona's narrative. Her pained words reflect her living sorrow:

My mother was always afraid I would get hurt or that something would happen between us because our love was so good. She could not believe that it would last. I do not see, in many couples around me, the kind of love that Jacob and I shared. It took me a long time, many long years, to recover. To this day I have never visited Jacob's grave. To me, he is not underneath the ground. He is inside me, inside my heart.

Benny dies shortly after this photograph is taken. This image of pure joy is marred, knowing what is about to happen to him. He tenderly cups his niece's small head in the palm of his hand as he lovingly gazes upon her. A week later, his life is gone. His own seed, his link to immortality, lost.

The familial features can be seen in their shared large foreheads, partially opened mouths, almond-shaped eyes. This brave, heroic soldier, humbled in the presence of new life, cannot foresee that his own life will soon be over, as hers is beginning.

These are the last photographs taken of Benny. The end of the frame. Down
the road and over the hill he meets his fate. He looks back one last time,
blond, curly locks peeking under his helmet, his hand positioned, prepared for
battle. Far in the distance, where the land meets the sky, where the cyprus
trees grace the barren land, waits the mortal fire that will crush his unlived
dreams, pierce his father's heart, and shatter his sister's life.

Rivkah

We saw Benny for Rosh Hashana. We could never have imagined a week later that he would be dead. Benny loved Israel, the army, his soldiers. His soldiers respected him. Not long ago, I met this man I had not seen for many years. We reminisced. He told me he would never forget Benny's laugh and strength, his love for adventure.

Benny's active service began in 1970. He had almost finished his duty. His friends completed their training but he volunteered for one more year. He was a commander and an officer. He was only 21 years old.

Benny was in high school when mother died. She came to Israel two years before World War II and lost her entire family in the Holocaust. He watched her slow deterioration from a brain tumor. Her death was a devastating loss and had a profound impact on him. Sensitive in nature, poetic, Benny was like a soft wind. After he died, my father published his book of poetry. Benny and I became very close after our mother died. All my friends became his and his friends became mine. After I married, my father and Benny came to live with us.

Tel Saki was surrounded. Over the radio Benny heard Menachem's desperate pleas. "Yaya," Benny begged, "we must help!" He could not bear to hear such cries. He beseeched Yaya. Yaya tried to persuade him that it was very dangerous, that he might not return. Benny said to Yaya, "These are my friends. I cannot bear it anymore. I want to go. I must go. I must try and rescue them!"

Yaya told my father that he gave Benny permission to go only with great reluctance and hesitation. He felt uneasy about the decision but Benny kept insisting, demanding, "I want to go. I must go." Benny could not bear it that his friends were suffering. Yaya gave him ten soldiers and two armored carriers. Even after they left, Yaya tried to persuade them to stop. After the war, they gave Benny the Medal of Honor.

GIDEON

I HAVE A NEWSPAPER ARTICLE written shortly after the war. A journalist describes the Tel Saki battle, the bunker and the soldiers who died. It does not mention the names of the soldiers who took part in the rescue mission nor how many of them died. He used a photograph, but only those who remained alive are pictured. Jacob is absent.

The people in the Tel Saki bunker knew that soldiers were coming to the rescue. In this situation, however, it was a suicide mission. Those in the bunker knew it was suicidal but are ashamed to admit it. Rarely is the Tel Saki story told from the point of view of the soldiers who came to rescue them, the soldiers who sent the reinforcements. No one likes to talk about this. What is heroic about this event? Show me one heroic deed attributed to the dead soldiers. The dead soldiers tell the whole story.

A few years ago I worked in an emergency room. Yaya came in with his wife. I treated his wife and asked Yaya, "Do you know who I am?" "No," he replied. I reminded him that I was one of his soldiers and Jacob Rayman's best friend. He knew Jacob Rayman. He knew the story, though at the beginning he said he did not remember. He did not want to talk about it, though there was no reason not to. The room was empty, I was not in a rush. But he changed the subject.

Who've huddled all together in the corner,
And press each other closer still and quake;
For here it was the sharpened axes found them,
And they have come to take another look,
And in the apple of each staring eye
To glass once more the picture of their end,
Of all the terror of their savage death,…

—Hayyim Nahman Bialik, *Night*

Chapter Nine

D E S P E R A T I O N

SHLOMO

MENACHEM TRIES TO OBTAIN PERMISSION TO LEAVE TEL SAKI. His superiors will not grant him this request, and order us to stay a few more hours. They need us to report the Syrian actions, and will give us the order when they receive this information.

By the time Menachem receives permission to leave, it is too late. He gives the order to retreat into the bunker. I have my Uzi but I cannot find my pouch. Later, I discover that one of the bombs fell on my pouch. I do not know why the Syrians did not enter the bunker, but if they had we would not be alive. Their soldiers made a mistake, and we who survived are lucky. This is all.

Inside, the bunker is dark and cramped. Matches can be used only in emergencies. Huddled together, Menachem and Eliezer pray in the dark. The Syrians throw in grenades. I try to protect my heart from being hit.

By night, we become desperate for water, as our soldiers lie dying. Most are seriously wounded and distraught with pain. Our nearly futile situation leaves no other recourse except to try to find water. And so I volunteer with another soldier to leave the bunker in search of water. We wait until the moon disappears and the night is completely black. Even a moving shadow can cause a skittish Syrian soldier on lookout to take pot shots into the phantom, ghost-filled air. Stepping out, our eyes quickly seize our goal. In the distance we see the outlined shapes of our abandoned burned armored carriers. We mentally estimate the distance and time we have left, knowing light breaks early in this high mountainous area. Syrian soldiers sleep nearby in various positions, their bodies looming like small dirt mounds, and often change positions as they try to find comfort on this rugged tel. We gingerly step over them, hearing pebbles, small rocks and broken gravel break away from our carefully-laid boot steps. Rumbled noise from these scattered rocks sounds like fully amplified echoes. I fear the noise can be heard from miles around and will wake the restless, sleeping bodies beneath me. Barely breathing, half walking, half crawling, we finally reach our goal.

To our great dismay and shock, the water container stored on the side of the carrier has been exploded by one of the Syrian bombs. With no other choice, we scoop the remaining water that has condensed at the bottom and put it in a small jar. Feeling with my hands, I find a small can of olives and a box of crackers. I know I should feel grateful, but instead I feel an overwhelming disappointment and concern. I do not know how I can stretch this tiny offering.

The darkened sky protects us as we start our journey back. Great mountain ranges far in the distance beacon a kinder world. Still, cold night air momentarily sends a shudder through me although I am wrapped warmly in my army jacket. Night sounds, like a rustle from a stalking bird or snake, can be heard as we crawl back. I fear our moving shadows will suddenly trigger suspicion among the Syrians on night watch. I pray silently to myself. The box is bulging under my coat. We do not have much more time and I am grateful when we finally reach the bunker. Moaning softly, eyes closed, whimpering "Imma" in resigned whispers, our soldiers find no rest. I grind the crackers into smooth crumbs and carefully parcel them out to each soldier. Otherwise, the crunching might wake up and alert the Syrians stationed directly outside the bunker entrance. I open the small container of water and pour a precious amount into the container's tiny cap. With one hand I lift each soldier's head, bring his mouth to the edge of the cap, and let him lap the water like a cat.

The road to Tel Saki is badly damaged with potholes. To drive on it becomes a test of endurance, machoism and risk. This bare, unequipped, concrete bunker became the refuge for Menachem's group and more than two dozen stragglers from other units. It had no water, transmitters, food, telephones, first aid or artillery. Nothing. It is a miracle a bomb did not explode the entire thing. Even though most of the soldiers were parched and desperately wounded, they were forced to maintain the code of silence.

In war, courage is parcelled. Brave acts are propelled by Divine Will. Survival is measured in moments and hours. Terror sweeps into the hearts of these remaining, huddled few.

ELIEZER

WE WATCH AS TWO ISRAELI ARMORED CARRIERS ARRIVE with our soldiers, and pray fervently for their safe arrival. And as they jump out, one by one, falling like matchsticks from the mortal coil, our hopes collapse, our spirits break, seeing senseless, evenly-timed slaughter mow down the best of our generation.

I hear later that four of these soldiers survive this carnage, escape to Tel Saki and hide behind our bunker. They hear the bombs and grenades, decide not to come in, convinced no one remains alive.

The Syrians are suspicious when it becomes completely quiet, and send more tanks. More bombs. One of these bombs badly wounds many of us, especially Menachem. Desperate, our bunker becomes like an open grave that we have been thrown into after being maimed and shot, abandoned and given up for dead. We are not even a cohesive group. A straggler from one unit and a soldier from another, no one knows to whom they belong or from whom they are to take their orders. I do not know any of these soldiers.

Our communication is destroyed, our radios are broken. Sunday evening, a soldier remembers that one of the Israeli armored vehicles has a working radio, so Shlomo and another soldier from the tanks crawl around sleeping Syrians to search for it and bring it to Menachem. Menachem contacts his commander, Yaya, and tells him that a few of us remain alive. Astonished by this news, Yaya promises us that help will come soon. Hope bursts into the air for the first time since the war began. But it is short-lived. We have a severe water shortage. We make do with some dry cracker mix that tastes awful. None of us feel we will be alive by morning. Every moment that passes brings us one minute closer to death. Each breath is labored, and reminds me that it may be my last. We have to be completely still, though everyone is seriously wounded and in desperate pain, crying and dying.

AVIGDOR

FOR ME, THE WORST MOMENT IS MONDAY MORNING, October 9, when we lose the entire area. Each moment seems like hours. I feel like we have lost our lives and our country.

YAIR

I SEARCH AROUND WITH MY HANDS. Hundreds of Syrians dot the tel, posing and squatting leisurely, like satiated lions following a successful hunt. I have fasted on Yom Kippur, am losing a lot of blood and do not know what to do. Hallucinogenic water mirages appear in the distance, and thoughts of waving my hands to the Syrians to ask for water do not seem bizarre. It is at this time that two Yairs begin wrestling for command of my thoughts: logical Yair and irrational Yair.

Irrational Yair, desperate for water, wants to throw caution away, but logical Yair demands attention. "No. Wait until night." Four hundred meters ahead lies a charred vehicle and I decide to crawl toward it, concluding that there must be a container of water. Terrified, I know if the Syrians see me they will shoot. I remember thinking that the speed of a bullet is faster than the speed of sound. If I will be shot, at least I will not hear or feel the act. Strange thoughts gained possession of my mind during this extreme period of intense fear. Impossible behavior takes on great magnitude, and seemingly impossible actions suddenly make complete sense. The desire to live convinces me that unless I try to reach the burned car for water, there will be no hope of surviving.

The greatest difficulty arises when I try to turn 180 degrees. Crawling without barely moving, crawling without making a sound, crawling without being detected by the Syrians peering through their binoculars at the human debris below, demands my total concentration.

Sometime toward early evening I reach the tank and crawl underneath its rails. Imploring, I pray to survive this war in one piece, that God in all His infinite mercy will bring me water and that He will provide me with the strength to crawl to the Kinneret. And then I turn my head. Only thirty meters from me stands a long line of Syrians patrolling, ready to shoot. I must have looked suspicious. To this day I am not quite sure what I did. Maybe I raised my head, maybe a sudden spastic movement caught the attention of a soldier standing nearby on high alert. Whatever it was, he took notice and started walking toward me. He had a high chin and

forehead and a small moustache. He flashed his rifle as he briskly walked towards me. Coming closer, I feel his footsteps pounding in my ear, my heart racing, convinced he can hear the beating of my heart thumping against the ground. I clutch my gun tighter. The army has taught me well. A soldier must never abandon his gun—we go to jail if we do—and instinctively I bind myself to it, gaining false power from its strength. Abruptly, it is completely quiet. Just as suddenly loud shooting shatters my eardrums. My left side explodes in agonizing pain. I open my left eye—my right is sealed shut from sticky, caked blood—and I swallow. I can swallow! I move my leg. My leg moves! Ahead, the soldier is walking away! I stare at his back. Maybe he senses a presence of life from this stare, like invisible electrical currents that pass through two human beings, because he turns around, picks up a rock and throws it at me. I hear the sound of the rock hitting my helmet. I am sure it is a bullet instead.

The Syrian is breaking a rule of war taught during army training. On patrol during battle an enemy soldier is to be shot and killed, not left. The enemy soldier could be alive and, during an off-guarded moment, attack and shoot. Instead, he throws a rock. Like an Ish from the Bible, this soldier gives me my life.

Soon complete darkness falls upon this wasteland, this open graveyard, this land of death. I stand but keep falling. Nerve damage has created vertigo in my ears and I cannot maintain proper balance. I locate the jerry can but it is empty except for a centimeter of water lingering in the bottom. I lift the can to my mouth and say a prayer over the water. "Be quiet or the Syrian will say amen," I conclude. My humor remains the only familiar trait I have left.

Day breaks. I hide behind some large rocks. Throughout the long, sun-drenched, dry day, I lean, half-standing and half-sitting, and watch our planes battle overhead. Long stretches of time disappear as dizzy blackouts take over and I fall into unconsciousness. Rows and rows of Syrian tanks continue to travel west. "How far are they getting?" I sadly wonder. Tiberias? Haifa? In my fragmented imagination, I see children with their parents heading toward the beach, the Syrians following in close pursuit, as the few remaining survivors are swallowed by the sea.

The Syrian tanks continue, like a constant stream of killer ants. I realize it is foolish to remain where I am, and decide to move from the path to avoid being sighted.

MENACHEM

THE SYRIANS KEEP THROWING GRENADES INTO THE BUNKER. In a bunker of this size, the shrapnel results in each of us being seriously wounded or killed. We lie with corpses, awaiting our fate. The surrounding darkness mirrors our souls and undermines what is left of our strength. I order the soldiers to stifle their cries. Not to talk. We must play dead. For an entire day and night we do not move or speak. This silence burdens us. We have no water, little food, barely any ammunition, serious to desperate injuries, much loss of blood and no way to escape.

Small miracles seem to make themselves known in dire circumstances. In our case the Syrian soldiers, who are standing so closely to the entrance that we can hear them arguing, decide not to enter.

I am forced to send Shlomo and a tank soldier into the night to try and find some food and water from the burned vehicle. Weighing this decision, I decide that if the Syrians sense our moving figures, they will have no reason to believe we could be Israeli. They probably assume they have succeeded in killing all of us.

Our need for water is critical. In the tank, Shlomo discovers a small container of olives. I will never forget swallowing these crushed olives. It felt as if a life-saving intravenous tube had been inserted into me and was pumping the soft olive liquid through my veins.

I pray silently in the corner while most of us lie dying. Shaya Levy, close to losing his mind after a grenade has shattered his eardrums, shouts for water. Crazed by pain he shrieks for help, each time alerting the Syrians who respond by throwing in another grenade. I keep hissing to be quiet but he cannot hear or understand me. I finally have no alternative. I cannot allow his cries to kill the rest of us. My mother, the only member of her family to survive the Holocaust, suddenly appears in front of me. I remember a story she shared from long ago: Germans were searching a home where Jews were hiding under the floor. A baby began to cry, and the mother was forced to smother it. Her presence reminds me of this story, and I realize that I have no choice but to order this hard decision. I give the order to Eliezer to strangle Shaya. He tries to strangle him but fails. Paralysis has set into his badly damaged hand and he cannot apply pressure. At this moment, Shlomo solves our dilemma with brilliant insight and nerves of steel. He takes apart one of his cigarettes and writes on the paper, "Do not shout. There are Syrians outside. We do not have any water!" Swiftly, he holds the fire from his lighter directly in front of Shaya's burning eyes, then clamps the lighter closed. As delirious as Shaya is, he understands. We do not hear another sound from him.

SHLOMO

SHAYA SAW A SMALL CONTAINER OF WATER I had brought in from the outside, and because of his severe wounds and hearing loss he kept yelling, "Avital. Water! I need water!" I kept whispering to be quiet.

After his failed effort, Menachem finally orders me to strangle Shaya before his shouting gets all of us killed. At this instant, out of nowhere, an idea occurs to me. Impulsively, I take apart one of my cigarettes and write on its paper, "SHEKIT! BE QUIET! THERE ARE SYRIANS OUTSIDE AND YOUR YELLING WILL GET US ALL KILLED IF YOU ARE NOT QUIET!" I grab my cigarette lighter, hold the paper in front of one of Shaya's eyes and just as quickly put out the light. In hindsight this was foolhardy and risky. I was lucky because it could have backfired. A fire from a lighter flickers and creates moving shadows upon the walls. The Syrians outside could have seen this and would have known we were alive.

After Shaya read the note he became very quiet. He was fortunate I smoked in those days because had I not, I would have strangled him. I am not quite sure I would have been able to live with myself today, but I would have done it. And I believe that, in reverse, he would have strangled me as well. It was not just my life. There were other soldiers, too.

ELIEZER

IT WAS NOT UNTIL MONDAY that the IDF began its offensive against the Syrians. We waited in terror, fearing that the Syrians would explode more bombs at Tel Saki in their retreat. Instead, they began searching for shelter to protect themselves from the Israeli bombs. They came to our bunker. They were so close, we heard them speaking directly outside the entrance. They could not decide whether or not to enter. At the entrance, they saw dead Israeli soldiers propped in a sitting position. When they saw these Israeli bodies, they began arguing with each other. Was someone alive inside the bunker? How did dead soldiers sit propped against the wall if there was not someone alive inside? Was this a trap?

We kept absolutely still. If they came in we were prepared to throw our grenades. We pulled out the pins and held our breath. The tension almost snapped our nerves. Wound like coil, we were ready to spring. After minutes of argument they decided not to enter and left. We collapsed from the sheer strain. Two hours later another group of Syrians arrived. It was the same situation, the same argument. They also left.

Between these two events, the episode with Shaya occurred. He was severely wounded, could not hear, his arm was broken and he was very weak. I do not remember any order by Menachem to strangle him. Shaya does not remember either. I lay near him when he awoke, and he began crying for water. I instinctively tried to quiet him. Because my right hand and arm were broken, I put my left hand to his mouth and said, "Shhh." He caught my broken hand and began to twist it. I tried not to shout but went berserk with pain. It was difficult to pull away from his tight grip.

Menachem may have given me the order to kill him but I was in too much pain to pay attention. I do not know if Shaya read Shlomo's note or just slipped into unconsciousness, but after the note he was quiet. Later, when I heard this story, I told Menachem I did not try to strangle Shaya. I would not have been able to do this. No one would have been able.

SHAYA LEVY

THE SYRIANS LAUNCHED A MISSILE TOWARD THE BUNKER. One of our soldiers died instantly. I was hit in the head, arm and shoulder. I lost consciousness. After the war, I heard all this talk about them trying to choke me, but I do not remember any of it. In the hospital, they asked me if I recalled groaning, crying or making noise. I do remember screaming and yelling because I was in much pain and fear. I knew I was losing a great deal of blood, and I felt that I was dying. My dangling finger was cut to the bone and I recall being mesmerized, playing with it in a detached kind of way. I did not know what I was doing. I remember watching water being served. At times, I think I remember someone trying to choke me, but I am not aware if this is because I have been told the story. I do know that Shlomo saved my life.

War is a messy business.
Actions often hide motivation.
Decisions are made on the spot.
Second guessing comes only later.
Recriminations.
Self-doubt.
Guilt.
This is the material of hindsight.
During the war, in the war, it is different.
One simply does without thought.
Like an animal, an animal instinctively
trying to survive.

—Anonymous

Chapter Ten

THE TENSION IS BREAKING US ALL

The Past:

Murky Syrian shadows stand outside. Arabic floats through our cramped quarters, hammering fear into our hearts, like nails pounding into brand-new coffins. Rough army blankets bruise our open wounds. The stench of putrid vomit and rancid, soiled fatigues fills our nostrils. Ready, like taut bows and arrows we wait for the signal to remove the pins and release our grenades. Coming from behind what seems like a flimsy curtain instead of thin concrete, low Arabic voices filter in like poison gas.

The Present:

The deserted abandoned bunker leans precipitously against the tel. Tossed into the valley below, like discarded litter, it remains surrounded by old barbed wire and debris. The bunker space, hardly large enough for a small handful of soldiers, once held five times this amount during the war. A new bunker has been resurrected where it once stood. Land-mine warnings dot the barren landscape as soldiers patrol, rehearsing for possible war.

SHLOMO

A SMALL VENTILATION HOLE IN THE CEILING created a major dilemma
for me. I imagined myself standing in the boots of a Syrian soldier, knowing that if I were one of them I would look for a hole like this. I feared
that the Syrians would throw a grenade through this hole and finish us off
once and for all. I removed my helmet and placed it over this opening. If
they did throw a grenade I would lose only my left hand. Since I am right-
handed, it would not be a horrendous loss. I held the helmet in this position for a long, long time until I lost feeling in my arm and simply could
not hold it any longer.

The Syrians kept throwing in grenades. They made a direct hit. I took
two of my grenades, removed their pins and came close to throwing them.
If I had, I would have started screaming, revealing to them that we were
alive. The tension was breaking us all. They kept throwing grenades and
shooting inside the bunker. We had to play dead when we all were in great
agony, when it went against what we instinctively wanted to do. From
where I sat, I could see where they stood by the entrance. Most of us lay
crying. We knew this to be the end.

ISAAC NAGARKER

I WAS ONE OF THE LONE TANK STRAGGLERS who found his way to the bunker at Tel Saki. Most of my unit had been wiped out by the Syrians. I did not know anyone in the bunker and no one knew me. A soldier left the bunker and went out to the Syrians, screaming that inside all were dead. I do not know if he was waving a white sheet or not. I would assume that he was, but it did not matter. We all heard the shots and then the silence. It was at this moment that something broke inside me. Maybe it was looking around and seeing everyone barely alive. Maybe it was the corpses. But I felt only despair. Our only hope was to stop the constant barrage of grenades that the Syrians kept throwing inside the bunker. I looked around and saw that I was the only one standing. I was not hurt. I did not discover until later that my leg had been wounded. There was no one but me who could leave the bunker. Maybe I stood a chance. I knew that the grenades were killing everyone and that, if the Syrians continued, there was no hope that anyone would survive.

I did not allow myself to realize that I faced either death or a Syrian prison and torture. I saw only the desperate circumstances that we were in. I braced for the worst and stepped into the night darkness. Things happened fast. I screamed, "ALL ARE DEAD! I AM THE ONLY SURVIVOR!" Guns raised, pointed at me. Yelling Arabic. Too much yelling. More Arabic. Commotion. Too much chaos to feel fear. That came later. Suddenly, I was thrown to the ground, blindfolded, my head smashed with the butt of a gun. Later, I learned the reason why I was not killed. In the dark my tank uniform looked like a pilot's suit, and pilots are always taken as prisoners of war because they carry information.

They handcuffed me and beat me badly. My leg began to hurt. They gave me water to drink because I was losing so much blood. From there I was taken in and out of various army vehicles, and finally I was dragged on the ground the last few kilometers to Damascus. I was nearly killed by a stampede of Syrians when they learned that I was an Israeli. In prison, they put a cast on my leg which they then ignored, and my leg began to rot.

The Syrians did not let in the Red Cross. During interrogation I was badly tortured, deprived of food and sleep, and kept in solitary confinement. My filthy, tiny cell was freezing cold. I was covered with lice and bugs; they crawled inside the cast and nearly drove me mad. Rats never left. Toward the end, I was able to obtain information about Tel Saki. I was told everyone died. My family was told I died. From inside the bunker, the soldiers thought I had been shot. But no one could find my body. No one was sure. I was in prison for nearly one year and came close to dying many times. I was released in a prisoner of war exchange. The cruelty of the Syrians was unimaginable. It is too difficult to speak. Forgive me.…

I do not feel it took courage to do what I did. I had no choice but to try and deflect the Syrians from the bunker. I am grateful to speak openly about my experience. This has given me relief. Many soldiers still suffer from shock. I do not. One reason is that I share my trauma when I am asked to speak to different army units. This has made all the difference.

Yaya

MENACHEM

BARELY ALIVE, WE HANG ON BY A THREAD. Every twenty minutes I whisper to Yaya, "Please. Please rescue us."

"Menachem," he whispers back, "stay alive for only twenty more minutes. Please. I am with you. I am coming with the entire IDF. Do not give up now." Little did I know that he was completely alone, hiding in a dark field, so close to the Syrians he can hear them breathing. His regiment is battling near Tiberias but he has decided to stay behind just to remain in contact. He does not want us to feel abandoned. He keeps pretending he is coming with the whole IDF. The big, huge IDF. We keep thinking he is showing up in just another twenty minutes. We desperately need hope and he is giving it to us, like a life line thrown into a deep, dark, dry well.

He lies to us for more than 24 hours. We so want to believe him that we do. Why would Yaya lie to us? Twenty minutes pass. I stall another twenty minutes before I phone again. I fear bothering him too much. He is major of the entire regiment, and after all it is war. "Menachem. The men are changing their tires. We are coming. Can you not hear them?" And he creates noises like men changing tires as he hides alone behind desert shrubs and rock. And I continue to believe him. Twenty minutes and we will be rescued, I repeat to myself like a mantra. Twenty more minutes. I only need to hang on for twenty more minutes. If twenty minutes is all that it will take to save our lives then we will hang on. I repeat to my soldiers under my command, "We must hang on. We will be rescued in only twenty more minutes." If Yaya had told me the truth—that we were completely isolated in the Golan Heights, surrounded by thousands of armed Syrians, that no one was close to us at all, that we were totally alone, and that the best estimation of any IDF rescue would be at least 24 hours, possibly 48 hours—we would have died. His lie gave us this incredible power and strength to stay alive.

Of steel and iron, cold and hard and dumb,
Now forge thyself a heart, O man! and come
And walk the town of slaughter....
The black, dried blood, commingled here and there
With brains and splintered bone....

Outside, the sultry air is thick with feathers,
And thou shalt think to wade as in a river,
A flow of human sweat, the sweat of anguish....

They're just whole lives of men, whole lives of men,
Like broken potsherds, past all mending ever—...

—Hayyim Nahman Bialik, *Night*

Chapter Eleven

R E S C U E

Shouts. Curses. Moans. Boots shuffle against dry, rocky dirt. Cracks from distant fire. Shouts. More shouts. Pounding. Rifle butts smash against the bullet-riddled walls. Banging. Random stray bullets burst nearby. Yelling. War-weary reserves deplete borrowed strength and break through the blocked entrance. Drumming. Six-point-star choppers quickly swallow our half-dead, the dangling, the open-eyed.

Clean-up. Wordless soldiers sweep the corpses that are strewn around like rotten debris. I fear finding my friend among these scattered bodies and know but for a stroke of chance go I. In this valley of death, I see my reflection in each muted face. Uncomprehending eyes stare back. Six-point choppers rumble in the distant sky. Silence. And then, more silence.

MENACHEM

MONDAY, AROUND NOON. At a certain moment, without warning, I hear steps. We try to hide. We are sure of another grenade. And then we hear shouts, soldiers speaking Hebrew! We know then that it is over. Our rescuers are in shock that any of us remain alive.

SHLOMO

EVERY TIME I HEAR A SOUND, my heart races. Monday morning, eleven o'clock, I hear Hebrew! Rescue! They first evacuate the wounded. I discover my legs have been hit by a grenade and that one leg is broken. The entire time I am in the bunker I have felt nothing. Only later do I discover I have permanent hearing damage.

ELIEZER

EARLY AFTERNOON, the IDF finally arrives. The doctors immediately send us by helicopter to the hospital.

SHAYA

WHEN RESCUE COMES they ask me if I can walk. I fall. These soldiers who have come have shown great courage.

ITZHAK

BADLY WOUNDED ALL OVER MY BODY, I lose too much blood. My sealed right eye causes an imbalance in my equilibrium. At this time I do not know that my sight from this eye is finished, like a prism of a thousand lights splintered into a million pieces. Water remains for only one more day. We fear that Benny is dead. We cannot make communication and we do not know what has happened to his men. Later I learn that eight soldiers die in the first rescue and five in the second. Three of the original ten are now with me. Two succeed in joining Menachem.

Sunday night. We decide if we are to have any chance at all we had better try and evacuate the area. Barely alive, we wait for the moonlight to disappear. Around two in the afternoon, we crawl very slowly toward the main road. It takes more than an hour. I collapse. I can go no further. A soldier remains with me, and Meir and another soldier leave to get help. All night we stay by the road. By Monday morning I begin to lose hope. Syrians keep passing. I become convinced that it is the end of Israel. I break down sobbing. Even though I am not religious, I pray deeply. We stay like this without any visible protection. By Monday noon, I know I am dying. I have no more strength. And then we see the Syrian tanks retreating! Hope suddenly looms for the first time! The Syrians are leaving! Late afternoon, we are rescued by the approaching IDF troops.

MEIR

BY NIGHT, THE SITUATION IS EXTREMELY GRAVE. Itzhak's severe injuries, along with the other soldiers' wounds, demand that we act immediately or we will have no chance of survival. It is crucial that we let the IDF know the gravity of the situation. We wait impatiently as the full moon rises in the sky. Only when it finally descends do we begin our journey. Half crawling, half walking, we struggle for two hundred meters. And then we stop. Itzhak and the soldier cannot go on. Their wounds and gravely weakened states make it impossible. A fourth soldier and I decide to hide them, walking and crawling the remaining 12 kilometers without them to seek help. I leave them my last water bottle. We struggle through the area that is now under Syrian control until we reach our troops and I meet up with Yaya. He thinks all the soldiers at Tel Saki are dead. I inform him that there are some survivors. Late Monday night I find an unused jeep at the base and drive back to the spot where I left Itzhak. He and the soldier are not there. I search for him and discover Itzhak at a hospital in Tiberias and the other soldier at a hospital in Afula. After the offensive began, they were rescued. I am relieved and grateful to find them alive.

YAIR

THE ENDLESS COLD NIGHT batters my broken body. Each second I feel myself closer to death. It seems less and less something to fear and more and more something to want. My dizziness saps my strength. My thirst makes me desperate. Far ahead, rows and rows of Syrian tanks keep marching forward. In an Arab country, is it better to fall captive with the infantry or with the tanks? I decide it will be better with the tanks because a tank gives protection. Soldiers in infantry are on the run, tense, and will shoot from nervousness. Holding my broken rifle I take what feels like my final breath and brazenly start walking toward the tanks. Dragging myself is more like it. I stand, then fall, then totter forward, forcing my bloodied, damaged body onward. I know I cannot survive much longer without water. I cannot put my rifle down because it gives me strength.

Thirty meters in front of me I am looking directly into the cannon of a tank. For days I have been wandering alone, without food or water, thrown against rocks, burnt by the sun, terrorized by Syrians, and now in my final moment it all comes to this uneventful end. Mesmerized, delirious, I cannot take my eyes off the cannon when suddenly I recognize Hebrew lettering. I see an Aleph! This is Israeli! This is our tank! A rush of energy bursts forth and I start snapping my fingers, dancing, like Tevya from *Fiddler on the Roof.* An Israeli soldier with sideburns—which immediately tells me that he is from the reserves—steps forward and comes toward me. Soon a jeep follows with paramedics and the following day I am in the hospital.

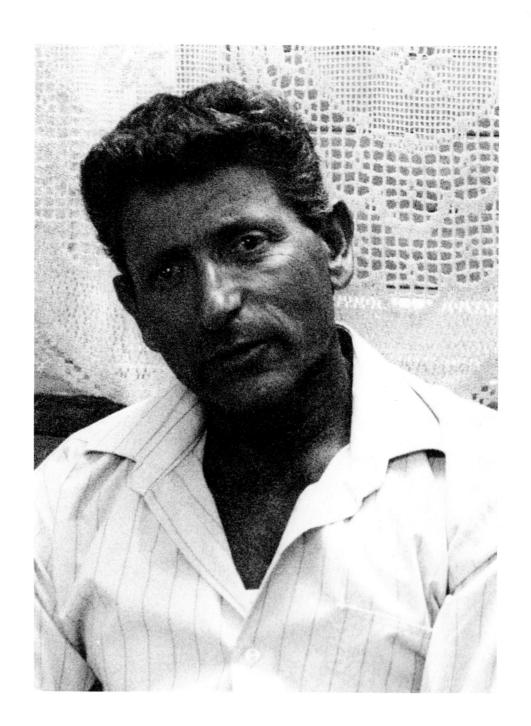

ESHEL EHUD

DURING THE WAR I WAS AN INTELLIGENCE OFFICER in the tanks. Stationed
in the southern part of the Golan Heights, one of my many duties was
processing information. The situation was extremely grave. I remember
midnight Saturday, the first night of the war. We were desperately trying
to refuel and reload our tanks following a brutal attack by the Syrians. We
came across Yair's armored carrier waiting in ambush on the road to Tel
Saki, near the junction of Ramat Magshimim. We urgently told his driver
that Tel Saki no longer was in our hands, that it was now Syrian controlled. "Do not go there," we argued, trying to protect our fellow soldiers.
For nearly an hour we tried to convince them to stay where they were, but
they refused to listen. They responded that their commander, Yaya, had
ordered them. Yaya was my friend, so I tried to radio and confirm this
order. It was to no avail; I could not locate him. And so we parted.

Monday afternoon, we receive instructions to go to El Tamora. I do
not remember the time. I recall we were on a road on which we had not
received permission to travel. I do not remember who saw him first, but a
soldier appeared from behind a rock and a field of dry bushes. The red
kafiya Arab scarf wrapped around his head indicated that he was Syrian.
There he stood, twenty meters from the main road, with one of our soldiers posed to shoot, when I decided he could be useful for interrogation.
"Do not shoot! Do not shoot him!" I ordered. Later, I was asked by my
commanding officer how I could see this man from twenty meters away.
How could I have failed to see his gun? "Maybe it was tucked behind
him," I responded. I do not remember if he emerged from the bushes
dancing. When I approached, he was by the road completely still. He was
in bad shape. He hardly had strength to stand, let alone attack. In fact he
had to be carried to the truck for questioning. Only at this point did I
observe he was an Israeli from the parachutes battalion, that the red Arab
head-dress was a scarf deeply bloodied from serious head and neck wounds.

Monday night, the Syrians attacked. Badly injured, I was flown to
Afula hospital. My right eye lost, with shrapnel in my mouth and bones,

pain ransacked my entire body. At the beginning, I was bedridden because the operations sapped my strength and I was in a great deal of torment.

A week after my surgery, I was resting with other soldiers in the dining room when one of these soldiers started telling me the story of what had happened to him. I was listening, not paying much attention, when suddenly I realized that this soldier was talking about me! "That was me!" I exclaimed. "I am the one who picked you up. I am the one who rescued you!" So here we were, in the same hospital, our eyes and faces wrapped and bandaged, neither one of us able to see the other, and I hear this story being told of my rescue by the very soldier whose life I had saved!

Yair

FOUR DAYS AFTER I AM ADMITTED TO THE HOSPITAL, a soldier named Ehud is assigned nearby. Both our eyes and faces are bandaged, so neither one of us can see. With nothing to do we begin talking to each other. He asks me if I want to hear a strange story.

He had been in the southern part of the Golan Heights when he was radioed that a Syrian had been spotted stepping out from thorn bushes alongside the road. Ordered to shoot him, he hesitated. As an intelligence officer, he decided he might be able to obtain information from him instead. He ordered his soldiers not to shoot.

As this Syrian approached the tanks, he noticed that he was acting peculiar—waving his hands, snapping his fingers—bizarre behavior under the circumstances. To avoid frightening him, he felt the safest approach would be by foot. Walking slowly yet deliberately, he discovered upon closer inspection that he was an Israeli, had been in the parachutes division, and had been wandering alone in the fields for days without food or water. The Syrians had given him up for dead after hitting him with their rifles, kicking his body and throwing stones at him.

"This was me!" I exclaimed to this soldier I could not see. "You are telling me my story! I am the soldier whose life you saved."

Most melancholy at that time, O Friend!
Were my day-thoughts,—my nights were miserable;
Through months, through years, long after the last beat
Of those atrocities, the hour of sleep
To me came rarely charged with natural gifts,
Such ghastly visions had I of despair
And tyranny, and implements of death;
…Death-like, of treacherous desertion, felt
In the last place of refuge—my own soul.

—William Wordsworth, *The Prelude: Book Tenth*

Chapter Twelve

RECOVERY: THE YEAR FOLLOWING THE WAR

This photograph, taken just before the war, tells the story of war. The soldiers sit, relaxed and smiling for the camera, in a long row. Little do they suspect that, in less than a week, half of them will be dead.

Of the soldiers in this photograph, the first dies. The one sitting next to him lives. The third one dies. The fourth one lives. The fifth one dies. The next one lives. Dies. Lives. Dies Lives. Dies. Lives. From this image, how random is death. Yet, on the other hand, it says just the opposite: death is not random at all, everyone's fate has already been sealed before the first bomb ever exploded.

MENACHEM

I REMAINED IN THE HOSPITAL for many long months. Slow and painful, my complete recovery took nearly a year. The first few months all I did was sleep. I could not bear to lie awake. I endured terrible nightmares and still bear permanent scars. Emotionally, I have not recovered. The experience continues to haunt me, and I avoid and withdraw from intimate contact.

ITZHAK

IN THE MONTHS AFTER THE WAR, I would suddenly begin sobbing. I still am not fully recovered from my wounds. As time passes, my suffering becomes increasingly internal. I do not think much about the war, yet I never stop grieving. We failed, yet we almost succeeded in our mission to reach the bunker. I am proud we did not retreat in our rescue. On this point there is no doubt. We fought hard and did our best to save our friends. We did not leave behind any bodies of our soldiers. We knew how to shoot and how to operate a blended car. In this catastrophic situation, we did not give up hope. Myself, Menachem and the few who survived were only lucky.

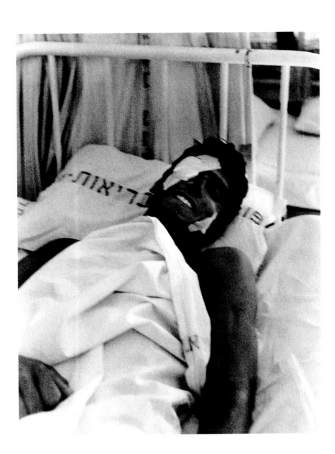

ISAAC

AFTER MY RETURN TO ISRAEL, I was told that the Syrian government released a fuzzy photograph of me to Israeli authorities. By then my hair was long, I had a beard and had lost more than 25 pounds. Based on the picture, many families claimed me as their son and urged the Israeli military to release my name. Maybe there had been a mistake. Maybe their son was missing in action. Desperate, hoping beyond hope that their son had not died but instead had been taken as a prisoner of war, many parents held onto this photograph as mistaken proof that their son had been captured rather than buried in a makeshift grave.

In the army, body identification is not made by parents since it is often too personally devastating. Because of the number of casualties during the Yom Kippur War, temporary graves were used until permanent grave sites could be prepared.

Hope against hope. Possibility against impossible acceptance. Families created chaos in the hallways of the military information centers. Parents screamed and cried to each other, tearing and clutching at my photograph, looking for vague markings as confirmation that the soldier in the picture was their own son. This photograph, this unclear black-and-white image, was their evidence, the only available proof that their son was alive and not buried in a lonely grave.

ELIEZER

AROUND THE TIME OF MY BAR MITZVAH, I read a book about a 13-year-old who had a special Bible that he was saving for 120 years. I did not believe at that time that something like this would happen to me. I only know the following story from the doctor who operated on me.

During the High Holidays a special prayer book is used. Because I am religious and the war broke out during Yom Kippur, I had it with me. When I was ordered to Tel Saki I placed it in my breast pocket located over my heart. This prayer book is extra thick because there are more prayers to recite on this holiday. At the hospital, the doctor threw my clothing to the side so he could immediately cut and remove the bullet and shrapnel from my chest. When he removed the bullet he became suspicious about how I could have survived such a direct wound to the heart. He suspected something must have slowed the impact from this particular kind of bullet. He went exploring to find the answer for himself, and began searching through my bloody clothes.

One day he brought me my prayer book. Soaked in my dried blood, the bullet had penetrated the book, fanned out and stopped one millimeter from my heart. I would have died had I used my regular daily prayer book because it is much thinner.

I now understood the story of the Bar Mitzvah boy who was saving his Bible for 120 years.

He gently dislodges the prayer book from its sealed zip-lock bag, as the memory floods forth, gasping for breath. The book's torn and weary pages now hang loosely in its frail binder, the old, stiff glue worn thin. So small, the book can fit easily into the palm of his grown hand, yet so thick it cannot disappear. The book stands alone, confident and clear in its message, with a quiet inner dignity, proud, so proud that its meaning has been tested and proven true. He handles the book with a holy reverence, as if the book itself is the prayer. And indeed it is.

Shlomo

For years, we soldiers spent 24 hours a day together, showering, sleeping in the fields, patrolling, eating. We were closer friends with each other than with our friends back home. My best friends ever were from this period. I will never stop missing them. We shared war, the most intense experience of my life.

After the war was over, I visited my friends who survived. But in a short period of time this became too hard. All I could see were the ones who were not present. More than half our group had died. All we had in common were memories, memories that were too painful. I withdrew from all contact with anyone who reminded me of the war.

After the war, I could not talk or think about it. I tried to prepare a scrapbook but I could not complete it. I had trouble concentrating and focusing. Finally, I threw all the souvenirs and photographs from the war into a box and placed it in the farthest corner of a closet. I never looked at it. This included the watch that I wore during the war, that my father gave to me on my Bar Mitzvah. I never wore it again.

It is hard to believe that more than a quarter of a century has passed. My wounds are raw. I am still not healed.

Yair

For weeks after the war I lay in the hospital, tormented by nightmares. In the army they had taught me how to run, fight and win, but during the war I failed at all of them. Now, alone with my guilt and devastated by the loss of my best friends, I knew I needed conventional therapy but decided instead to treat myself.

I returned to the Golan Heights to find solace and answers to why I had survived and my friends had not. Every night I walked alone under the black, empty sky. During the war it had been the night that had protected me. Now I screamed like a hurt animal, howled like a wolf. If anyone had seen or heard me they would have thought me mad, but I never felt this way. I felt out of control when I would remember what I had lost.

A year after the war, on one particular evening I was walking alone in a field when I found myself reluctantly returning to the feeling I had when I was caught. Suddenly overcome by a strange exhaustion I stopped, unable to take one more step. I do not know what triggered this emotional paralysis, but this experience became a defining moment in my recovery. I finally understood that I had to stop asking questions about why I survived. I had to accept the fact that I lived. There was nothing else to do.

Yaya stands planted on the rock, as strong as a tree that spreads its roots below and gathers nourishment from hidden water wells. Like the broken half of a six-pointed star, the remaining friends and family members gather together a year after the war to remember their loved ones who fell at this desperate battle.

Directly in front and center, a woman looks away, her grief permanently etched into her face, like a road map that leads nowhere but here. Two children, unable to fully comprehend the anguish of their family, sit quietly. No one speaks.

Harder to imagine is that here the land was fertilized by tears and cracked by shovels, that haunting remains were deposited in the not-so-distant past. Worn paths disappear, then reappear several yards away. Undercurrents of air gently blow, lifting sand particles and carrying them far into the distance. A young soldier perished on this rock where his parents now stand.

The blood has dried. The bodies removed. A year has passed. Only volcanic black rock remains. And an unending grief.

Even in our sleep, pain that cannot forget falls drop by drop upon the heart, and in our own despair, against our will, comes wisdom through the awful grace of God.

—Aeschylus

Chapter Thirteen

WAR REFLECTIONS: 25 YEARS LATER

Vigilant, anonymous tank soldiers protect their sacred country—Eretz Israel. It was not always this way. Jews had no country to call their own, as roots cannot take hold in foreign, hostile soil.

May 14, 1948. Israel became a state with a flag, language and army. For the first time in a millennium Israel had its own army and land. Without this land there is no freedom. The Jew can walk proud, stand strong, defend him or herself against world-sanctioned slaughter.

Soldiers march onward to engage the enemy before the enemy annihilates them. There is no choice. Silhouetted, nameless, these sculpted Jewish soldiers continue on their war road, determined in their effort, committed in their zeal, believing in their mission, to the end of life or death.

Menachem

When we retreated into the bunker, I promised my men that if we survived I would throw a party. Deep inside my heart I knew I would not have to fulfill this promise. I told Yaya that we would not see each other again. I knew it to be the end. I ordered the final procedures. We burned maps, codes and all materials we did not want to fall into Syrian hands. From the time we entered the bunker, we were completely and totally isolated.

At twenty years old, I was a year older than the soldiers I was commanding. I was placed in charge to rescue and protect them, to give answers I did not have. I still question if I could have done better, if I could have acted differently. The torment always begins when I focus on the question that still remains unsolved: Why did the Syrians not enter the bunker? This question leads me to my self-doubt. Could we have crawled into the valley and tried to reach Israel through the canyon? Should I have warned our soldiers not to rescue us, to go back? My commander did not know any other way to rescue us, and he could not dare allow himself to think that he would leave us abandoned and alone. I remain as shocked by what I did do as by what I did not do. Everything feels connected to me and everything remains incomplete. I feel God's protective Hand because I am alive, but what would Jacob say? Did the soldiers who died feel God's Hand, too?

So much for me remains unanswered. Why did the Syrians stay and fight us? They lost too many hours and did not move on until Sunday afternoon, when they had to face our reserves. If they had not stopped they could have conquered Israel. There was not one single soldier between them and our country. I wish I could meet with the Syrian soldiers who fought at Tel Saki. I am curious to know how they perceive and understand the battle. I would like to ask them if we succeeded in convincing them that we were many. Did they think we were dead? How did they interpret the sight of our two blended cars? Did they think there were more in hiding? Why did they not enter the bunker?

Tel Saki is a famous battle for the IDF. It is taken as an example of the spirit of our army. I am most proud of the first half of the fight, of how we delayed the Syrians and prevented them from penetrating Israel. We were only five men and two armored rescue carriers of twenty that stopped an army of a thousand. We were so few against so many. Most of us died.

The battle is more famous for the second half, and it is this half that I am most ashamed of. We only tried to save ourselves. We did not do anything for our people or Israel. We, who were there, do not feel like heroes. We feel the opposite. I have heard that one of the soldiers tried to commit suicide. Another soldier went mad and had to be institutionalized. One would expect that the survivors would have a reunion once a year, but we do not.

After the war, a commission was assigned to determine why we were so unprepared. The chief of staff was fired, along with some generals. It brought down the government in power. New rules were enforced, especially in regards to Intelligence. On one hand we gained confidence. In this terrible, unprepared situation we still did not lose. On the other hand, we are less confident and more fearful that we will face another war. We have been taken off the pedestal as the great Israeli warriors. Our enemy no longer fears us.

ITZHAK

THE ESSENTIAL QUESTION ASKED by the families of the slain soldiers is: Why did we not order Menachem to leave, to run away Saturday night before he was surrounded? Our mentality does not allow for this kind of thinking. Trained not to abandon a strategic point, Menachem would not leave until the order was given. I believe the higher commanding officers did not understand the gravity of the situation, the sheer number of Syrians.

More than 15 of our soldiers fell on the rescue operation. Soldiers died trying to save other soldiers. Why did Benny go without Intelligence information? Why was he not more careful? I think he felt he had no choice but to do the best to save his friends. They fled so quickly, they fell into a trap. Menachem feels the Syrians thought Israeli soldiers were waiting in ambush behind the tel, and that this is what stopped them from continuing to Tiberias.

Questions remain unanswered. How did our fight at Tel Saki impact the Syrians? Did it delay their advance? Did we succeed in giving the impression that we were stronger than we were? What did they think of our fight? Why did they not move directly to the Kinneret on Sunday morning? Maybe our two blended cars did stop the Syrians and did keep Israel from losing the war. The answers to these questions would tell me if my friends died in vain. But we will never know.

Before the war we had a feeling—and it was wrong—that nothing could happen to us, that our enemies would not dare start a war. We were deadly wrong. This mistake changed all of our lives.

ELIEZER

TEL SAKI WAS THE MOST TERRIFYING EXPERIENCE OF MY LIFE. I was 19 years old and had not yet begun to live. Only now, when I can look back, do I see the life experiences that I would have missed. My severe injuries from terrible stomach and hand wounds caused much suffering. Fragments from a bullet smashed my teeth, yet this same bullet prevented shrapnel from penetrating my mouth. I did not suffer from nightmares like so many others. In the bunker, I feared for my mother. My father had died two years earlier and I knew that she would not be able to live with my death. It would have destroyed her.

After the war, Menachem kept his promise and invited all of us to his home. We shared our stories. After this meeting we never met again. What would we say to each other? Relive the story over and over? Menachem and I stayed in touch because we are both religious and have this in common. With the others, I have little.

Parents of the slain soldiers ask Menachem why he was not given permission to leave. Our commanding officers felt they needed more time to stall the Syrians, to mobilize our reserves. Nobody knew the exact number of Syrians to Israelis. Every minute was critical. It was our duty to stall, to stop them.

We were five soldiers, and more than twenty came to our rescue as thousands of Syrians waited in ambush. The chance of a successful rescue was zero. Why try this rescue? Nearly twenty of the soldiers who tried to rescue us were killed. And only one was killed from our five at Tel Saki. More soldiers were killed in the rescue than were lost at Tel Saki!

The IDF does not make a calculation by number. The army would not be what it is if it did. The conclusion drawn can never be fair. Every Israeli soldier knows in each situation that the army will do whatever is necessary to rescue him. It is this knowledge that keeps the morale.

The war fundamentally changed Israel. We lost faith in our heroes and legends, and confidence in our political leaders, as cracks in the IDF were exposed to the public. Most of the army is a reserve army. When we mobilize, the world knows. Six months before the war we had a mobilization that was a false alarm. It cost Israel nearly thirty million dollars, and the government was heavily criticized. Thus the government was cautious about ordering another mobilization on the heels of this fiasco. We did not want to give our enemies a reason for alarm and provoke them to war. It is easy to reevaluate the situation and to see our mistakes in hindsight.

Israel is our country. We must remain strong in spite of our problems. To be strong, we must continue to tell the real story, our story, the truth. Only in this way do we convince our young people to fight for their country, to die for Israel.

The war challenged my belief in God. It was not a difficult test because I was religious and survived. How many families of the slain soldiers believe in God? I finished this war feeling all was nonsense, that other than a few important, essential matters, most things in life are not worth dying for.

Shlomo

FOR MANY YEARS I TRIED NOT TO TALK or to think about the war. The army would phone and ask me to speak to the new recruits about Tel Saki. I did it a few times and then stopped. It became too difficult. We almost lost this war and in many ways we did. There were too many mistakes and careless decisions. Too many soldiers died. Unprepared, because of our arrogance and feeling of invincibility, we have no one to blame but ourselves.

Before the war I was indifferent to life. If I died, so what? After the war, I saw life through a different lens and realized how fragile I am. Now when I am in the car and see a young boy drive recklessly, I want to scream at him, "Are you crazy? Do you think your car can protect you? You can die in a second! Does a kiss or love mean anything at all?"

It is hard to believe that more than a quarter of a century has passed. My wounds are raw. I still am not healed. The war destroyed every illusion I had. I never regained my trust.

I was born in Morocco and my family moved to Israel in 1961. My parents named me after a famous Moroccan rabbi. I am one of six brothers and a sister. All my brothers served in the war. My father prayed to God, promising that if He let his six sons survive, he would go to the synagogue every week and leave food and clothing for the poor. Miraculously, none of his sons fell. My father kept his obligation to God for the rest of his life. I feel I honor my father when I continue with his obligation. My father felt God's greatest gift to him was keeping all his sons alive, that he did not have to bury any of his children.

YAIR

TEL SAKI CHANGED MY LIFE. After facing the Syrians, daily problems are easily kept in perspective. I choose not to talk about the war. Soldiers today are from a new generation, and to them the battle seems one hundred years ago.

When I remember Jacob my body shakes and the experience washes over me. The war remains close. It has taken ongoing self-examination to achieve the fragile equilibrium I maintain today. Some of the other soldiers who experienced Tel Saki do not feel the same way. They told me something broke inside. Their bodies have repaired but they themselves have not and never can. No one who fought at Tel Saki can ever be the same. In each of us, a part of ourselves died, a part of us shattered.

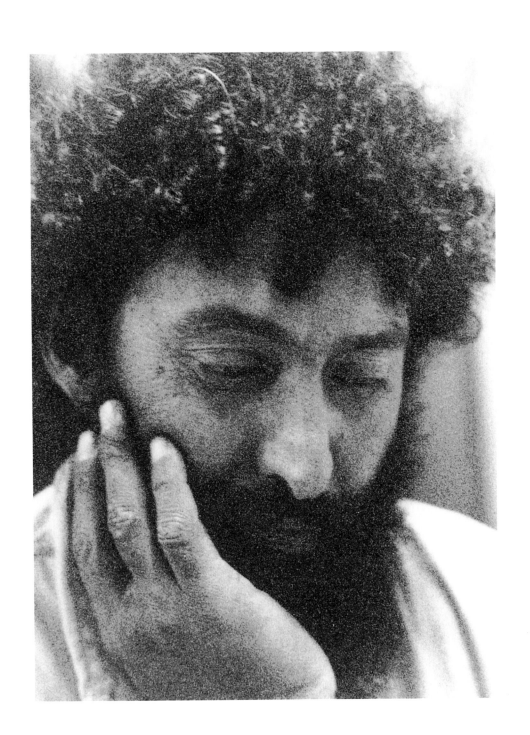

In spite of being surrounded by a warm, loving wife and four kind, attentive children, Shaya remains aloof, intense, brooding. Hard to engage, he spoke reluctantly about his war experience. The war left him permanently handicapped, necessitating a custom-designed, control-steering mechanism so that he can drive his car.

SHAYA LEVY

I ENDED THE WAR WITH PERMANENT HEAD WOUNDS and many injuries, from which I still suffer today. I lost my finger and much of my hearing. I do not have nightmares but, on the other hand, I never stop thinking about Tel Saki. The war never leaves me and I experience the impact from it daily.

I would love to know the soldier who shot the missile into the bunker that permanently altered my life. I witnessed the Syrians celebrating their success when they hit our tank. It filled me with an uncontrollable rage. Helpless, having no weapons or supplies with which to retaliate, defenseless, watching them reload and replenish their stock and manpower, left me powerless and with a feeling of fear that I live with today. When a terrorist attack occurs in Israel, I am forced to relive what happened to me.

The soldiers who tried to rescue us showed great courage, and I will always feel indebted to them.

The war was a grave mistake. I am not political, but the mistakes were politically motivated. After the war, I contacted the other soldiers, especially Menachem, but now I have nothing to do with them. The connection is gone.

GIDEON

ONE HUNDRED PERCENT OF MY LIFE WAS INFLUENCED BY JACOB. I followed his way. I joined the same Nahal group, became a medic in the army, went to medical school, became a doctor. Jacob became the symbol of how I wanted to live my life. I sought to be like him, to step into his shoes. My family and I even explored the places in America where he had lived. With most friends, there are aspects of them that are not admirable. With Jacob there was not one character trait that disturbed me. He was a success in high school, the army, with girls, and as a medic.

It feels as if Jacob died yesterday. Our relationship lasted five years but it seemed like twenty. I will never again have a friend like him. We were more like brothers. How often does a friend come along with whom you can share without being afraid, without fear of judgement, disappointment or anger? Once? Twice?

For me, it is hard to understand what motivated Morty and Ruth to leave America. He was successful, moved with his two children to a country at war, and had to start his practice from the beginning while already in his forties. They truly loved Israel. They feared Jacob would be drafted to Vietnam. They remained when most of their friends returned to the States. Even if they wanted to, how could they now leave their son whom they took to Israel and who was killed? We never talk about it but I cannot believe that Morty does not think about it. It is impossible for someone to accept. You take your son to Israel, and he is killed in a war for the State of Israel.

RIVKAH

MY FATHER WAS NOT DESTROYED BY BENNY'S DEATH, but his spirit was broken. I think this is why he died from a heart attack. Before the war he was filled with laughter and joy. After Benny's death he rarely laughed again.

On Yom Kippur my father walked to the Kotel, praying. Shrill, loud sirens erupted—the warnings of war—so he hurried home, passing armored carriers on the road. Gazing toward the heavens he prayed to my mother and pleaded with God to protect his son.

My brother's death profoundly changed my life and my children's lives. His death is with me all the time, in every decision I make. It affected the way I raised my children, and the size of my family. Even though we are religious and my six daughters did not have to go, they chose to serve in the army. The choices they made for themselves—the eldest becoming an officer—were a result of Benny's death.

His death taught me courage. I am able to let trouble flow from me. I do not keep problems churning inside. I have strength to draw upon; if I survived this I can survive anything. I have learned to pass my fortitude to others.

After Benny's death I became sensitive to events in Israel. When I hear about a soldier's death, I hear the same knock at the door. The knocking at the door. It sounds like no other. It disturbs all the world. Nothing will be like it was before. The knocking at the door. The silence. The car. The car engine turned off. The knocking at the door. In my final month of pregnancy I could not sleep and once heard a knock of a car door outside. I jumped, ran to the window and heard myself say aloud, "It has come back. The knocking at the door."

Moments return to haunt me. Two days after Benny died, my father and I sat in the Sukkah, speaking quietly. Suddenly we both began sobbing. This has remained the saddest moment. Benny's memory often is triggered by an incident. Benny's hair was curly blond. When I would see a blond soldier I would find myself chasing him. He would turn, and of course it would not be Benny. A deep, sad longing never leaves. My father once told me that he spoke to Benny all the time, every day, in private conversation.

YAYA

THE ATTITUDE TOWARDS THE DANGER OF WAR has changed because of
the peace agreement we made with Egypt. Egypt succeeded in surprising
us, and gained much advantage from it. They made a breakthrough in the
Yom Kippur War, and it was this breakthrough that brought us peace with
Egypt. It does not matter that we made a comeback—probably the greatest in all military history—or that we advanced victoriously from the
worst situation imaginable, penetrated Egypt, circled their entire army
and reached within sixty miles of Cairo.

The Syrian experience was the same as Egypt's. They took us by surprise, captured the Golan Heights and killed thousands of our soldiers,
until we managed to regain the Golan, reaching within twenty miles of
Damascus. Since 1973, Syria has been our quietest border. I think this is
the result of the Yom Kippur War. In spite of our success in 1973, we cannot forget that we faced the worst threat to our existence since the War of
Independence in 1948.

The Yom Kippur War taught us many lessons. We must pay attention to
our Intelligence. We must always be on the alert, strong at each moment.
We can never let down our guard, not even for a second.

AVIGDOR

THE YOM KIPPUR WAR CHANGED ISRAEL. It forced us to alter our habits, our mentality, the system. We have to monitor our enemies carefully, concentrate on our Intelligence, pay attention to details, be ready for combat at any time, and remain aware that every decision carries grave consequences. This war changed my mind about the enemy. We now live with the feeling that they still hope to beat us and that one day they will have the capability to do it.

We must spend more money and attention on the next generation. There is a saying in the Bible from King Solomon: "Generation goes, generation comes and Israel shall forever stay." It means that we have to protect the country from generation to generation. The Arab people do not accept us. Period. We are still fighting for our survival. During the war I had the feeling that we had lost the country. Most of my friends died. My brother was in the middle of his honeymoon, returned to serve and was killed. My wife lost two brothers.

I have two sons serving in the Golan Heights. Fighting for what I believe in gives me strength. I have found that people who have the courage to do something for their country have a different view of the country than those who do not possess that same fearlessness.

Racked by self-doubt in the past, I now feel whole within and comfortable with my ideas. I do second-guess, and have conflicts with myself, but this is good. I worry more about people who feel they know it all but who actually have no idea about anything.

People have forgotten how many lives were lost in trying to reconquer the Golan Heights.

We did not start the war against Syria.

To die...to die...so young to die...
no, no...not I.
I love the warm sunny skies,
light, songs, shining eyes.
I want no war, no battle cry—
no, no...not I.
But if it must be that I live today
with blood and death on every hand,
Praised be He for the grace I'll say—
to live, if I should die this day...
upon your soil, my home, my land.

—Hannah Senesh, *To Die...*

Chapter Fourteen

———————————————————

J A C O B

Hava Rembrand is a serious woman. Sad. There is no frivolity about her, no spontaneous joy. She is a devoted daughter to her elderly parents and a dedicated mother to her two daughters and one son, Yankele, who was named after Jacob and diagnosed as autistic at age four. I interviewed her a week after she and the children had returned to Israel permanently after living for five years in America. She had gone with her family to America in the hope of finding better care and educational possibilities for Yankele. She had not succeeded. Now, she has resigned herself to his condition.

Hava and I were not close growing up. To me, she was always Jacob's little sister, a vague background presence whenever he was around. We only began our own relationship after he died.

Over the years, I have developed a soft spot for Hava. She is well-guarded, defensive and almost impenetrable. Yet, there is something soft, kind and direct about her. She tries to be friendly, to reach out. Unlike her father, Hava is introverted. I respect her strength and modesty, her intelligence and seriousness, her unwavering devotion to her son.

For me, the greatest hardship of Jacob's death was taking on the burden of my parents' grief. The impact of his death left me trying to take his place—which of course I never could—and feeling the total responsibility for my parents. This is why I married young. I had to give them grandchildren since now I was their only child and hope. From the day Jacob died, they wanted a grandson named after him. This is why I endured so many pregnancies and miscarriages. I did not want my child to be an only child like me. I did not wish that on her. Jacob's death affected my whole life.

For me, Jacob's death is not felt daily. It is a different kind of loss. Its impact stems from what could have been. I am the only person in the world who had the same background as he, the same parents. Jacob and I were just starting to know each other as adults when we had our first conversations. I do think we would have gotten along even though we had different personalities. Jacob was exuberant, extremely interested in life, and he wanted to experience everything. He was much more of a daredevil than I ever was, more spontaneous. Growing up we were not close. I hardly knew him, he never talked to me, he was involved with his friends. But I adored him. The only time we shared was during family vacations. When I was little we played a game. He would roadblock me as I tried to go up the staircase. He would get on all fours and say "Roadblock!" and I would try to crawl over him. I was thrilled.

My girlfriends were in love with Jacob. His many girlfriends would try to get to him through me. When I turned 17, one of his friends became interested in me, and for the first time Jacob started to see me as a human being. This was just beginning to happen when he died. The loss for me is only what could have been.

During the war I served as a postal carrier. I do not know why I was home when I should have been working, but it was around ten in the morning and I was in the shower. Strangely, I had put on Jacob's bathrobe, which I had never used before, when I heard my mother screaming. I grabbed Jacob's bathrobe and rushed out just as my mother was throwing these men out of the house. I will never forget my mother's screams. My dad took my mother in his arms and they went into their bedroom. He motioned for me to follow. It was another ten minutes before I heard the news. I did not know if Jacob had been wounded, captured or killed. I just knew something terrible had happened.

The men who notified us did a good job. First, they knocked on the door of our neighbor, who told them that my dad was at the hospital and suggested they speak to him first, which they did. My father then joined them, and when they all arrived at the door my mother immediately knew. One of them was a nice, young American doctor. He tried to give me his telephone number, saying "If you need anything, a sedative, whatever."

We quickly moved into action. So many people had to be notified. My dad put a note on the door and closed his practice. "Sorry, no patients. Our son is dead." Word spread quickly. The house soon filled with food and people. We were not supposed to sit shiva because of Sukkot, but we had a minyan. My dad told my grandparents, then I had the job of caring for them. Thank God we did not have to worry about funeral arrangements. The first call I made was to Simhona. This was an awful job. I called my mother's brother. I barely knew him and neither one of us knew what to say. For the first time, I started crying. A friend of my parents saw my face, came over and hugged me. "You can cry, too, Hava. You can cry, too." I then returned to my job of taking care of everyone else. The next day my father disappeared to go off and fight. For the next two weeks we received an endless stream of people. I talked to them all, offered food and drink, translated Hebrew for my mother.

I felt my dad acted selfishly. I am not angry with him, but it was not fair to my mother. He promised my mother he would not do anything dangerous, but I think he ran off to get killed. I conclude this from an article I read in the Hebrew newspaper. When he applied for the position with the Surgeon General, a journalist in the room wrote that my dad said, "My son was just killed. Send me to the front line. I am a doctor. You need me." Later, I spoke to some people who knew him at that time. Most of the time they said he did not know what he was doing. I do not know how much good he did. I think they did him a favor by giving him the job; it was not that they needed him, but they could see that he needed them.

This tragedy taught me that anything can happen to anyone at any time. As for myself, I took on too much responsibility. It was not good for me. Jacob's death still looms as a big shadow over my life. I made many decisions that were influenced by Jacob's death, but if not this, I would have been influenced by something else. We are influenced by what happens to us. I used to dream that Jacob was alive and happy somewhere else, that he had been wounded and had decided not to return home. During his active service, he would come home, drop off his dirty clothes and rush off to be with Simhona. He always wanted to be with her. I felt disappointed and mad that he did not want to be with me. In my dreams, I am angry at Jacob for dying.

We were told a week after Jacob was killed. Usually families are notified immediately, and the funeral is held the day after. On one day, five hundred families were told. The soldiers' names were not in the newspaper because there were too many to list. The government claimed not to know who was alive or dead until they reconquered the area. Jacob's body was in a temporary cemetery in Afula. A year later we had the funeral in Jerusalem.

I do not know how much my parents' lives are shattered. They are old now and have problems from aging. For my mother, her loss has been a great part of her life. We are a close family and my parents have a good marriage. Jacob's death did not destroy their relationship. Nevertheless, they are deeply hurt and will never be the same.

Many families experience a loss of a child in this country. My loss as a sibling is not the same as my parents' loss. They will never recover from it. My loss is for the relationship that could have been. After the war, my parents tried to give their lives meaning. Menachem asked them to move to Maalle Adumim, which they did for many years. My dad tried to become religious, but it left him empty. I was in a therapy group for siblings, but I found it useless. Most of the kids seem to be angry with their parents for not giving them attention.

My parents have never regretted their decision to leave America and move to Israel. I feel it is better that Jacob died like he did than in an automobile accident. People die all the time for a lot less important reasons.

There are topics I do not discuss with my mother because she becomes emotionally tense over them. We never talk politics. We hardly mention Jacob. They have their own way of remembering him, and I respect this. I have come to a point in my life that Jacob is no longer the most important focus. For a long time he was. I want to focus on the living. Simhona is now a friend of mine aside from her connection to Jacob. For a long time my parents used to say, "We saw this friend of Jacob's and that friend of Jacob's. This one is doing this and that one is doing that. The memorial library this, the memorial library that." I went along with it. Now I am no longer interested.

I have given up trying to establish a connection between my children and Jacob. It is a shame. They know there was an Uncle Jacob, just like they know their great-grandparents, aunts, uncles and cousins died in the Holocaust. I am realistic now. I do what I have to do for myself and for my kids because I have no choice.

MORTY

BERATING MYSELF AFTER JACOB DIED CONSUMED ME. We dragged these two young people, my son and daughter, to Israel. We never asked them, "Do you want to go?" We said, "We are going." In retrospect we feel this was an important reason why we succeeded in remaining in Israel when ninety percent of our friends returned to the States. We did not say to ourselves or to our children that we were moving to Israel for a trial period. We said, "We are moving to Israel." Jacob ultimately felt that he had to be part of the decision, and this decision became very meaningful for him. I am sure Hava feels that same way. She has chosen to make it her home, even knowing it is harder for her family.

More than anything else, Jacob having fallen in war made me feel a part of Israel. I earned my badge. Years later, when Hava returned to America for five years to seek help and resources for her son, I was asked if my wife and I were now going to return to the States. This person was surprised to hear my answer. I told her I could not leave Jacob alone. She could not understand this. You have to lose a son to comprehend the depth of this kind of sorrow.

The greatest difficulty is when bereaved people do not grieve. Ruth never cried. I did not cry until six months later. We were on a fruit cargo ship in the Indian Ocean that was carrying oranges and grapefruits from Israel to Japan, talking about Jacob, when we both broke down. It was very important to be able to do this. It was really the only time that we did. Instead we have internalized his death. Many people observe all kinds of ceremonies to remember their beloved, to show memory and honor. There are anniversaries and Yahrzeit candles, kaddish. Somehow it never seemed important to us to do this. We never go anymore on Memorial Day when most people go to the cemetery. We often go by ourselves. We feel it is too personal, too individual. We go early, six in the morning, when we can be alone. We do not pay attention to the conventional milestones of grief. As far as we are concerned, we think of him all the time. We are always grieving. We think how he would have been forty now, a doctor, and married with children. Where are his children, the grand-children we would have loved? Every single day we remember Jacob. I see someone walking with the same gait or pose, and he turns around and it is not Jacob at all. It stabs you in the heart.

We were always hoping that maybe, just maybe there had been a mistake. That first year we were always hoping that they were wrong, that they identified the wrong body, that he had been captured by the Syrians, that they had the wrong information, that he would walk through the front door at any time. When the Israeli prisoners of war were released from Syria and were flown to our airport, we prayed that Jacob had been taken prisoner. We did not go to the airport, but one father did. When he finally realized that his son was not one of the soldiers, he went home and killed himself. I could understand his feeling.

I would give anything to trade places with Jacob. Anything. Yet, this is impossible to do. You cannot change places. I have lived my life. It is not right that I should be saying kaddish for my son. What father is supposed to say kaddish for his son?

What father?

קַדִּישׁ יָתוֹם.

יתום יִתְגַּדַּל וְיִתְקַדַּשׁ שְׁמֵהּ רַבָּא, בְּעָלְמָא
דִּי בְרָא, כִרְעוּתֵהּ, וְיַמְלִיךְ מַלְכוּתֵהּ,
בְּחַיֵּיכוֹן וּבְיוֹמֵיכוֹן, וּבְחַיֵּי דְכָל בֵּית יִשְׂרָאֵל,
בַּעֲגָלָא וּבִזְמַן קָרִיב, וְאִמְרוּ אָמֵן. קהל: אָמֵן

קהל ויתום יְהֵא שְׁמֵהּ רַבָּא מְבָרַךְ לְעָלַם
וּלְעָלְמֵי עָלְמַיָּא.

יתום יִתְבָּרַךְ, וְיִשְׁתַּבַּח, וְיִתְפָּאַר וְיִתְרוֹמַם,
וְיִתְנַשֵּׂא, וְיִתְהַדָּר, וְיִתְעַלֶּה, וְיִתְהַלָּל, שְׁמֵהּ
דְּקֻדְשָׁא, קהל ויתום בְּרִיךְ הוּא יתום לְעֵלָּא
(בעשי״ת וּלְעֵלָּא) מִן כָּל בִּרְכָתָא וְשִׁירָתָא,
תֻּשְׁבְּחָתָא וְנֶחָמָתָא, דַּאֲמִירָן בְּעָלְמָא
וְאִמְרוּ אָמֵן. (קהל: אָמֵן)

יתום יְהֵא שְׁלָמָא רַבָּא מִן שְׁמַיָּא, וְחַיִּים
עָלֵינוּ וְעַל כָּל יִשְׂרָאֵל, וְאִמְרוּ: אָמֵן.
קהל אָמֵן

יתום עֹשֶׂה שָׁלוֹם בִּמְרוֹמָיו, הוּא יַעֲשֶׂה
שָׁלוֹם, עָלֵינוּ וְעַל כָּל יִשְׂרָאֵל, וְאִמְרוּ:
אָמֵן. קהל אָמֵן

After Jacob died, Morty and Ruth mailed the following letter in response to the many letters they received from all over the world:

We appreciate your warm expressions of sympathy and your contributions in Jacob's memory. We would like to share with you a letter of Jacob's when ———— refused to volunteer for the paratroopers. Jacob's Nahal group sent him a letter of censor, and this is what Jacob wrote:

" ————, you demonstrated by your words an old technique. Instead of measuring up to a difficult problem you are evading it in that you and your friends are not willing to participate in the elite unit. You are ignoring the facts of the past and also of the present. If such a unit did not exist and there were no guys ready to take part in it then I doubt that you would have the opportunity to dream distinct ideals. The ideals are beautiful but our reality shows that this ideology is not enough and instead of dreaming we must stand on our feet and defend ourselves."

EPILOGUE

THE LEGACY OF THIS WAR was the Israelis' mistrust of authority and political leadership, a feeling of betrayal from the highest office down. Heroes were stripped of their aura and became flesh and blood. Cynicism replaced confidence. Anger replaced hope. Disillusionment shattered dreams. The idea of being a light unto the nation dimmed. Israel had been permanently changed. Unprepared and caught off guard, Israel's political leaders had consciously ignored intelligence reports given to them by their agents and generals, warning them that the neighboring Arab countries were mobilizing for war.

Israel won the war but the costs were so high that many see it as a loss. Israel was devastated, suffering three thousand deaths and more than 11,000 casualties in only 19 days—thirty times greater than the loss rate of Americans during four years of World War II. With a population smaller than greater Los Angeles, Israel has battled five declared wars in fewer than fifty years, in addition to two undeclared wars—the War of Attrition and the war in Lebanon—and ongoing, never-ending terrorism that eats into the heart of the country. Twenty-one Arab countries, Iran and Iraq seek to destroy her. Israel can never rest but must keep a constant vigilance.

And her soldiers—each soldier who survived did so with devastating battle scars and permanent wounds that could not heal.

BIOGRAPHIES
at time of interviews

Eliezer Agasi—Born in 1953, Eliezer entered the army after high school and was badly wounded in the Yom Kippur War. Upon graduating from college, where he studied economics and computers, Eliezer opened a software business. He is married and the father of three children.

Rivkah Ben Ahron—The older sister of Binyamin "Benny" Hanni, Rivkah lives in Judea/Samaria with her husband and six daughters. In honor of Benny, Rivkah's daughters elected to serve in the IDF, although religious obligation would have waved this requirement for them.

Menachem Amsbacher—After the war, Menachem landed a job as a bomb technician for the Israeli police and became part of an elite fighting force. He currently is part owner in Erez, a company that conducts research and development in field detection of drugs and explosives used in law enforcement. Married in 1975, Menachem and his family helped to created Maale Adumim, a settlement in Judea/Samaria. He lives there today with his wife and six children, the youngest of whom, Amichai, was named after the Russian aliyah meaning "The Return of Our People."

Shlomo Avital—Living near Tel-Aviv with his wife and three children, Shlomo received advanced graduate degrees in computer science. He currently works in computer programming.

Pinchas Berkovitch—Pinchas owns his own trucking company in northern Israel. He and his wife, a doctor, have three children.

Meir Brukenthal—Having served as a paratrooper in 1969, Meir advanced to operation officer as captain of his unit in 1974. Today he is a colonel, second in command of a brigade. He lives with his wife and six children on Kibbutz Hafet Haim, a religious kibbutz in central Israel, where he is in charge of the egg hatchery.

Eshel Ehud—In 1937, Eshel's parents traveled from Poland to Israel, where he was born in 1945 and later served three years in combat units. During the Six Day War, he served in the Sinai and Gaza, and in 1968 he became an officer and served in Intelligence. He was badly wounded in the Yom Kippur War. Married in 1968 and the father of four boys, Eshel lives in Kibbutz Terat Zvi in northern Israel.

Hanna Eliraz—Roni's sister lives with her husband and three children north of Tel-Aviv.

Yair Farjun —In 1950, Farjun's parents traveled from Tunisia to Israel, where he was born in 1953. He was inducted into the army in 1972, and returned to the the Moshav in 1975. Since 1983, he has been the southern area manager for Hevrah l'Haganat (Society for the Protection of Nature) in Israel. Married and the father of four, Farjun currently studies ecology.

Gideon Ginossar—Born in Haifa in 1954, Gideon's family moved to Jerusalem in 1969. From 1969 through 1971, he lived in Belgium, where his father was the Israeli attaché to the Common Market. In 1971 he returned to Jerusalem to finish school. From 1973 through 1976, he served in Nahal as a medic in the parachute brigade. Following his army service, Gideon studied medicine in Italy. He currently is a physician of pediatrics and internal medicine. He is married and the father of three children.

Binyamin "Benny" Hanni—Born in 1951, Benny became an officer at age 21. He died in the Yom Kippur War.

Roni Hertzenstein —Born in 1953, Roni died in the Yom Kippur War.

Avigdor Kahalani—During the Yom Kippur War, at the age of 29, Avigdor was battalion commander of the northern Golan Heights. After the war he wrote a best-selling book about war maneuvers and strategy that is used today by the United States West Point Academy and by the IDF as a critical study in tank warfare. He served for several years as a member of the Knesset and started his own party, The Third Way. He was one of the leading opponents of returning the Golan Heights during the Rabin/ Peres Labor government. In addition, he created Lutrun, a memorial between Tel-Aviv and Jerusalem that honors the tank corps and serves as a military museum and site for national ceremonies. Currently, Kahalani serves as a colonel with the IDF and is in charge of internal security as a member of the cabinet under Israeli Prime Minister Benjamin Netanyahu.

Itzhak Kahane—Itzhak is an engineer who lives with his wife and children at Kibbutz Gaash.

Shaya Levy—Shaya works for the Israeli military in security matters. He is the father of four children and lives north of Haifa.

Isaac Nagarker—Following his prisoner exchange nearly a year after the Yom Kippur War, Isaac returned to Israel. He lives in Qazrin, the only city on the Golan Heights, with his wife and four sons.

Jacob Rayman—Born in 1953, Jacob moved with his family to Israel at age 15. While serving as a medic in the IDF, Jacob fell in the Yom Kippur War.

Mortimer "Morty" Rayman—Born in Chicago, Illinois, Morty graduated Magna Cum Laude from Harvard, and received his medical degree from Columbia University. From 1953 through 1968, he was stationed in Europe as a captain in the U.S. Army Medical Corps. In addition, he practiced medicine in Seattle, Washington and was a faculty member at the University of Washington Medical School. In September 1968, Morty and his family moved to Israel. In 1973, following the death of his son Jacob in the Yom Kippur War, he volunteered for the IDF.

Hava Rembrand—Born in 1956, Hava graduated Cum Laude in Philosophy and Jewish Thought from Haifa University. From 1974 to 1976, she served in the IDF. Since then she has published numerous articles and spoken on autism, and has held the position of secretary of The Autism Society of America. Hava has three children, lives north of Haifa, and is currently a librarian.

Simhona Weber—Simhona is a biologist who lives with her husband and three children near Haifa.

Yair "Yaya" Yoram—Born in 1944 in Kibbutz Ein-Hanatsiv in northern Israel, Yaya grew up in Tel-Aviv. He was inducted into the IDF in 1963 and served in the paratrooper brigade, where he held every command position from platoon leader to division commander. During the 1967 Six Day War, his brigade broke through the Rafah strongholds in the Northern Sinai. He was severely wounded, but returned to command two months later. As a paratrooper battalion commander in the 1973 Yom Kippur War, Yaya successfully defended Syrian attack on the Golan Heights. In the 1982 Lebanon War, he commanded the paratrooper brigade that made the amphibious landing north of Sidon. His brigade breached terrorist and Syrian lines, and was the first to reach Beirut. In June 1992, he was appointed Director of IDF General Staff Manpower Branch, and in 1995 he was appointed military attaché to the Israeli embassy in Washington, D.C. He has devised a new method for training high-level command echelons, which is used in all IDF exercises and maneuvers. He is a graduate of U.S. Army Command and Staff College at Fort Leavenworth. He holds an MA in social and industrial psychology and a BA in psychology from Bar-Ilan University. Married since 1966, he has four children. His daughter, Shlomit, served as a captain and operations officer in the Israeli Air Force, and was killed in an aircraft accident in 1990.

GLOSSARY

A
Abba—father

Afula—town in Jezreel Valley

Aliyah—literally, ascending; emigrating to Israel

Amalek—In the Bible, Amalek was the first enemy to attack the Israelites after they left Egypt. King Saul also fought the Amalekites. The Biblical injunction never to forget the deeds of Amalek (Deuteronomy 35:17) became so deeply rooted in Jewish thought that many important enemies of Israel were identified as descendants of Amalek.

Assyrians—harsh Middle Eastern empire that reached its prime in eighth century B.C.E. and occupied ancient Israel

B
Babylonians—Middle Eastern empire centered in Baghdad that destroyed the first Temple and exiled the Jews in 586 B.C.E.

Banyas—national park on the Golan Heights

David Ben-Gurion (1886-1973)—founder and first Prime Minister of the State of Israel

Blended car—combination of a tank and a motor vehicle

D
Moshe Dayan (1915-1981)—Minister of defense during the 1973 Yom Kippur War, and chief of staff of the IDF during the 1967 Six Day War, Dayan, with his black eye patch, became a symbol of bravery and heroism, and was recognized internationally.

E
Eilat—resort city and port at the southern tip of Israel, located on the Red Sea and bordering Jordan

Eretz— land, as in Eretz Israel, Land of Israel, or the Promised Land

Erev—evening, or eve of, as in Erev Yom Kippur

G
Golan Heights—strategic overlook from which the Syrians, prior to the 1967 Six Day War, shelled Israel

H
High Holidays—Rosh Hashana (the Jewish New Year) and Yom Kippur (the Day of Atonement), which occur in the fall

I
IDF—Israel Defense Forces

Imma—mother

Ish—literally, man; often referred to in the Bible as a mysterious stranger, a phantom

J
Judea/Samaria—Biblical term for the territory often referred to as the West Bank; Samaria is in the north, Judea in the south.

K
Kaddish—mourner's prayer praising God but mentioning not one word about death, said daily after the death of a parent or child, then each year on the anniversary of the death

Kibbutz—collective settlement

Kinneret—freshwater lake in the Jordan Valley, also known as the Sea of Galilee

Kotel—Western Wall; remains of the exterior wall of the Second Temple in Jerusalem, destroyed by the Romans in 67 C.E.

M
Maale Adumim—suburb of Jerusalem, now a city of more than 25,000 people in Judea/Samaria providing strategic, defensive protection for Israel, built upon land conquered during the Six Day War. Zionists, believing that this land had been given to them by God, sought to resettle it.

Golda Meir (1898-1977)—one of the founders of the State of Israel and its first woman prime minister; prime minister during the 1973 Yom Kippur War

Minyan—quorum, consisting of ten Jewish males, age 13 and older, required for Jewish communal prayers

N

Nahal—1973 unit of the IDF whose soldiers lived on border kibbutzim where they worked the land and guarded the borders

Nagmash—light armored troop carrier

Negev—southern region of Israel

Numinous—God-inspired experience or revelation

P

Phoenix—mythical Arabian bird that lives to a great age, at which time it burns itself to ashes and, after three days, comes to life again; symbol of immortality, rejuvenation and resurrection

R

Ramat Magshimim—Jewish settlement on the Golan Heights

Rosh Hashana—Jewish New Year

S

Hannah Senesh (1921-1944)—Jewish Hungarian Zionist who lived in Palestine; at age 23, parachuted into Nazi-occupied territory during World War II, on a secret mission to rescue Jews and bring them to Palestine

Shabbat—Sabbath, lasting from dusk Friday until the third star appears in the sky on Saturday; commemorates both God's Creation and the freeing of the Jewish people from slavery in Egypt

Sheket—literally, be quiet

Shema Yisrael Adonoi Elohanu Adonoi Echad—essential prayer of Judaism, meaning "Hear O Israel, the Lord our God, the Lord is One" and signifying the Jewish people's faith in the Oneness of God (Deuteronomy 6:4)

Sherut—group taxi service

Shiva—literally, seven; the first seven days of mourning

Six Day War—1967 war in which Israel defeated five invading Arab armies in six days, reunited Jerusalem, captured the Golan Heights, the Sinai desert and Judea/Samaria

Siddur—prayer book

Sukkah—temporary structure first used by the Israelites in the desert after the exodus; built by Jews during the festival of Sukkot to commemorate the harvest festival and their wanderings

T

Tel—Arabic for a small hill with archeological remains

Tel Saki—small hill located two kilometers from the Syrian border and 13 kilometers from the El Al Israeli army base

Tevya—well-known character whose life inspired many stories by the great Yiddish writer Shalom Alechem

Tiberias—city in Northern Israel on Lake Kinneret

U

Uzi—automatic weapon designed and manufactured in Israel; first used in the 1973 Yom Kippur War

Y

Yahrzeit—Yiddish term for the anniversary of a death

Yiddish—language and culture of Eastern European Jews

Yom Kippur—holiest day in the Jewish calendar on which many Jews fast and refrain from work; the Day of Atonement

ACKNOWLEDGEMENTS

BRINGING A PROJECT LIKE THIS TO COMPLETION DEMANDED PATIENCE. I encountered obstacles in researching material and tracking down the soldiers connected to Tel Saki. Carrying camera equipment, traveling from city to city, moshav to kibbutz, seeking directions, navigating transportation in a foreign language, and interviewing more than thirty people in a country faraway required the assistance of many people.

In telling the story of Tel Saki, I decided to focus on the soldiers directly connected to Jacob and Menachem. I have not used the exact words of the soldiers, but have paraphrased the interviews in my own words. The words are my own, but the spirit and thoughts are the soldiers' experiences. I have tried to record the soul of what they shared with me. Since spoken English is completely different than written English, I have taken the liberty of interpreting their deeply felt sentiments with my own style of poetic prose. Italicized text indicates my voice.

I am deeply grateful to the many soldiers who opened their hearts and gave me their trust. In time of war, life and death decisions are made in an instant. In hindsight, one has a tendency to judge, to second-guess whether the decisions were right or wrong, or if the outcome of the war would have been different had these decisions been otherwise. No one will ever know. Unless one stands in the boots of the officers, who feel the pressures and fears and who bear the ultimate responsibility, no one can or should judge. A special thanks to Yair Yoram, Avigdor Kahalani, Meir Brukenthal and Menachem Amsbacher.

I returned to Tel Saki repeatedly to photograph and capture the terrain in different light. A warm thanks to Itzhak Kahane, who accompanied me to Tel Saki and walked me through the events. And to Uzi Ualdi for his invaluable assistance.

Dealing with the bureaucracy and security of the Israel Defense Forces was not easy, but I owe a special thanks to Colonel Uri Algom, in charge of the IDF and Defense Establishment Archives, Photography Unit. Most soldiers gave me unlimited access to their photographs. These images were in terrible condition, worn by time. They allowed me to take their only copies, trusting that I would return them. This gesture touched me deeply, more than they realized. Their photographs enabled me to try to capture their feelings in the photographic essays.

A special thanks to Morty Rayman, who gave me his encouragement; without his approval, this project would never have been completed. In America, the photographic material could not have been assembled without the skill and talent of my photography editor, Eric Poppleton. I also want to thank Sam Abell for his guiding support. And a special thanks to my friends at Silver Lab. Ruth Frank, Rita Frischer and Mary Katherine Parks Workinger provided invaluable editorial assistance. Monica Castaneda supplied fine secretarial assistance. Thank you to Michi Toki and Steven Jenkins of Blueprint for their care in handling this project, and for providing the book's elegant design. A special acknowledgement of appreciation is extended to the Israeli Consulate of Los Angeles, Rabbi Allan Schranz and Rabbi Levi Meir. And to the teachings of C.G. Jung.

My deepest appreciation, however, is extended to my family. My husband, Cary, understood what is involved in bringing a project like this to completion. I am grateful for the love and granite support that he has given throughout our years. His commitment to this project was unparalleled, and his input was creative and true. To my daughters, Yael and Rachel, who share the same passion and love for their Judaism and Eretz Israel as I, and a special thanks to Yael, who was instrumental and invaluable in her editing skills, suggestions and commentary. They encouraged the project even though their mother was absent for periods of time. The love of my family sustained me.

To all and to the many, I am forever in gratitude.

Hallie Lerman